MW01254847

Christian

DOCTRINE

A PENTECOSTAL PERSPECTIVE

VOLUME ONE

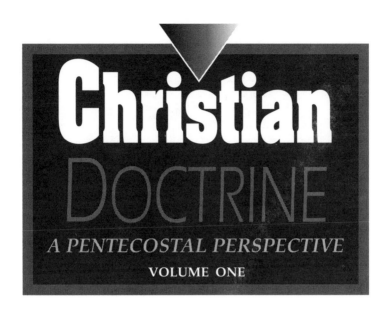

Christian
DOCTRINE
A PENTECOSTAL PERSPECTIVE
VOLUME ONE

FRENCH L. ARRINGTON

CLEVELAND, TENNESSS 37311

Library of Congress Catalog Number: 92-060723

ISBN: 0-871481995

*Dedicated to the women who have
influenced my life and ministry the most:*

Robbie Mae French Arrington, a Spirit-filled mother

Evangelist Ruth Baldwin Staples, my first pastor

Frances Lee Treadaway Arrington, a devout and
Spirit-led partner in matrimony and ministry

Athena Ann Arrington Hicks, our daughter, an
example of a Christian of great personal integrity

About the Author

French L. Arrington, an ordained Church of God minister, attended Lee College and graduated from the University of Tennessee at Chattanooga. He earned his Master of Divinity and Master of Theology degrees from Columbia Theological Seminary. His Ph.D. in Biblical Languages and Pauline Studies is from St. Louis University.

A respected Bible scholar and teacher, Dr. Arrington has served his denomination as a pastor, and Lee College as professor and chairman of the Department of Biblical Studies. He is the author of many journal articles and several books. He contributed articles to *The Complete Biblical Library* and edited *The Full Life Study Bible*. Among his books is *Acts of the Apostles*, published by Hendrickson Publishers.

At the present Dr. Arrington is professor of New Testament Greek and Exegesis at the Church of God School of Theology. He is married to Frances Lee Treadaway; and they have two children, Athena and Lee, and two grandchildren, Travis and Trent Arrington.

GENERAL
TABLE OF CONTENTS

Foreword

Pathway Press is pleased to present this first volume of *Christian Doctrine: A Pentecostal Perspective.* The author, Dr. French L. Arrington, is in his own right an authority on Scripture and Pentecostal beliefs. We expect this book to serve the church well as scholars, students, clergy, and laity use it to better understand and appreciate the Pentecostal perspective of Christian doctrine.

This first volume, on the doctrines of the Scriptures and Revelation, God, Creation, and Man, will be followed by two companion volumes. Volume two, on the doctrines of Christ, Sin, and Salvation, is tentatively scheduled for publication in the summer of 1993. Volume three, on the doctrine of the Holy Spirit, the Church, and Last Things, is tentatively scheduled for publication in the summer of 1994. An index to all three volumes is planned for the last volume of the series.

In addition to the author, many others have had a part in bringing this work to publication. This Pathway Press project began some four years ago under the general directorship of Dr. Floyd D. Carey and Editor in Chief Hoyt E. Stone. It is being carried forward to completion under the general directorship of Dr. Donald T. Pemberton and Editor in Chief Homer G. Rhea.

From the inception of this publishing project, Dr. Daniel L. Black has served as in-house editor for the publication of the three-volume series on Christian Doctrine. Critical reviewers of this first volume were distinguished churchmen Dr. David Lemons and Dr. James A. Cross, both now deceased, and Dr. William A. Simmons, assistant professor of New Testament at Lee College.

It is the belief of the publishers that this and the following volumes in the three-volume set on Christian Doctrine will be of service to the church at large for many years to come.

Homer G. Rhea, Editor in Chief
Church of God Publications
Cleveland, Tennessee

Preface

Christian Doctrine: A Pentecostal Perspective is a basic exposition of the Christian faith with an emphasis throughout on the vital role of the Holy Spirit in the life of the Christian and in the worship and ministry of the church. It is intended to enhance the church's proclamation of the whole gospel. It is also hoped that through the use of this book, laity, clergy, and ministerial students will grow in their understanding of the "faith which was once for all delivered to the saints" (Jude 3) and that they will fully experience the power and life made possible by Jesus Christ and the outpouring of the Holy Spirit.

This book is a biblical and practical presentation of Christian doctrine. Its theological orientation is decidedly Pentecostal. However, the author is aware that, among those who call themselves Pentecostals, there is a very broad spectrum of doctrine and practice. Therefore the term *Pentecostal*, as it is used in this work, means classical Pentecostalism. Classical Pentecostals, in addition to having their roots in the Wesleyan and Holiness movements of the previous two centuries, teach that subsequent to conversion the believer should be baptized in (filled with) the Holy Spirit, and that the initial evidence of this experience is speaking with other tongues as the Holy Spirit gives the utterance (Acts 2:4).

Pentecostal believers have much in common with the faith and practice of other Evangelical Christians. Nevertheless, the Pentecostals' experience and understanding of the Holy Spirit in the life of the individual Christian, and in the life of the church as a body, have prompted them to give a distinctive witness of life in the Spirit, which has helped form their understanding of the Christian faith.

This first volume of *Christian Doctrine: A Pentecostal Perspective* deals with those doctrines which should, logically, be first in order of study—the Scriptures and Revelation, God, the Creation, and Man. Unless noted otherwise, all Scripture quotations in this work are from the *New King James Version* of the Bible.

The author expresses appreciation to Dr. Floyd D. Carey, who, as general director of publications at Pathway Press, commissioned the writing of this work, and for his encouragement. Special thanks to Dr. Daniel L. Black, editor of Adult Sunday School Curriculum at Pathway Press, for his careful reading and editing of the manuscript. My wife, Frances, was also extremely helpful in reading the manuscript and offering suggestions for improvement of style.

French L. Arrington
Church of God School of Theology
Cleveland, Tennessee

COMPLETE
TABLE OF CONTENTS

Part One:

DOCTRINE
OF THE
SCRIPTURES
AND
REVELATION

Chapter 1

THE BIBLE

Pentecostals have been called "people of the Spirit," but they are also characteristically "people of the Book." *From their beginning, Pentecostals have had a biblical focus and have been led by the Scriptures as well as by the Spirit.* For Pentecostals divine truth may come in song, testimony, sermon, or through spiritual gifts, but all such means lead back to the Scriptures. Pentecostals see the Bible as more than a book of religious truths or a book that records God's works among ancient people. The Bible is a witness to God, but it is also the voice of God speaking across the ages. An encounter with the Scriptures is an encounter with the living God.

Convinced the Scriptures are God's Word, Pentecostals uphold the authority of the precious written Word and accept it as completely trustworthy for faith and conduct. This view of Scripture forms the basis for the Pentecostals' doctrinal statements and for Pentecostals' living in the Spirit. The Pentecostals' view of Scripture is informed by their experience of God's Spirit.

Terminology

A number of terms are used by Christians to speak about the sacred Scriptures. Prominent among these are the following.

A. Bible

The Scriptures of Christianity are gathered into a single book, known as the Bible. Derived from the Greek word *biblion*, meaning "roll" or "book," the word *Bible* came to refer to the sacred books (see Mark 12:26—"book of Moses"). The use of this term points to the fact that the Bible is made up of many books. Our Bible is a unique collection. In it we have the record of "the faith which was once for all delivered to the saints" (Jude 3).

The Bible is not a collection of ideas of great religious thinkers but a witness to what God has done. The Old Testament bears witness to God's mighty acts in Israel's history. God did no greater work for Israel than deliver them from Egypt. The Old Testament prophecies and God's mighty works prepare the way for the New Testament. They all find their full meaning in God's mighty saving deeds in the life, death, and resurrection of Christ (cf. 1 Corinthians 15:3-8). The Gospels tell of the life and ministry of Christ. The Book of Acts tells how the early Christians, after being endued with power at Pentecost, went forth with the message of salvation. In the Epistles the writers reflect on what God accomplished in Christ. The Bible tells the one story of redemption.

B. Scripture(s)

Literally this term means *writing(s)* and appears in the Bible in both the singular and plural. When it is singular (Scripture), the Old Testament is conceived to be one book, that is, a collection of inspired documents. For example, "All *Scripture* is given by inspiration of God" (2 Timothy 3:16). What is in view here is the Old Testament as the authoritative Word of God (cf. John 7:42; 10:35; Galatians 3:22). The plural (Scriptures) is used when the Old Testament is thought of as consisting of a number of documents (see Matthew 21:42; Luke 24:27; Romans 1:2). "The *Scriptures* of the prophets" (Matthew 26:56) implies the authoritative character of the Old Testament as a whole. Along with the other Scriptures, Paul's epistles are recognized as the authoritative Word of God (2 Peter 3:16).

C. Word of God

The Bible is God's Word—truth given by God. As such it is God's communication of divine truth. God uses a number of means to communicate or reveal Himself to us. The Bible is one means, but it is a special means because the Bible is God's Word. Recognizing this, Jesus distinguished between the Word of God and human tradition (Mark 7:13). Paul referred to the teaching of the Old Testament as "the word of God" (Romans 9:6). *God's Word is a message of His saving grace. This message of salvation is what the early Christians preached after the outpouring of the Holy Spirit at Pentecost and what God himself confirmed by signs and wonders.* The preaching of the Word of God by Paul and Barnabas was accompanied by miracles and led to saving faith (Acts 13:6-12; cf. 2:22; 10:38). "So then faith comes by hearing, and hearing by the word of God" (Romans 10:17).

Old Testament and New Testament

Our Bible is made up of two collections of sacred writings.

The Old Testament (the Scriptures of the old covenant) consists of 39 books, beginning with Genesis and concluding with Malachi. The Old Testament contains books of history, law, prophecy, poetry, wisdom, and apocalypse. The New Testament (the Scriptures of the new covenant) is comprised of 27 documents, beginning with the Gospel According to Matthew and concluding with the Book of Revelation. In the New Testament there are Gospels, history, epistles (letters), and apocalypse. The Old Testament is the Word of God given to the Hebrew people (the Jews) before Christ came, and the New Testament is God's Word given to the church after Christ came.

The basic structure of the Bible is that God made two covenants—the covenant of the law with Israel at Sinai through His servant Moses (Deuteronomy 5:1-5; Galatians 3:19) and the covenant of grace with Christians through Jesus Christ (Hebrews 8:6-13; 1 Timothy 2:5). Christians have a "better covenant" (Hebrews 8:6), but in no way does the new covenant of grace invalidate the Old Testament. The Old Testament is still the inspired Word of God "and is profitable for doctrine, for reproof, for correction, for instruction in righteousness" (2 Timothy 3:16).

Distinctives

Pentecostals believe the Bible is the most wonderful and helpful book in the world. As God's Word it cannot be classed with ordinary books. Convinced of this fact, Pentecostals go to the Bible with a firm trust in it. The Pentecostals' experience of the Holy Spirit has deepened their respect for the witness of the Scriptures, and the Bible is a living book to them. The Holy Spirit has led Pentecostals into a keen appreciation for the Bible as God's inspired Word.

A. Purpose of the Bible

Scriptures serve God's purpose of providing a record of

what God has done in the world for the salvation of all people. To be more specific, the purpose of the Scriptures is to testify of Christ (Luke 24:25-27) and to make us "wise for salvation through faith which is in Christ Jesus" (2 Timothy 3:15). The New Testament was added to the Old Testament in fulfillment of the promise that the Holy Spirit would guide us into all truth about Christ (John 16:12-15). God gave both the Old and New Testaments to promote the salvation of the world. Christ died and arose again, fulfilling prophetic Scriptures so that repentance and remission of sins might be preached in His name to all nations (Luke 24:46, 47).

The intent of the Scriptures is not only to lead us to saving faith in the person and work of Christ but to preserve and strengthen our faith (John 20:31; 2 Peter 1:19), to guide us in holiness of life (Psalm 119:9; 2 Timothy 3:16, 17), to give consolation in our afflictions (Psalm 130:5; Romans 15:4), and to provide us with spiritual weapons to combat error and maintain doctrinal purity (2 Timothy 3:16). Therefore, as our supreme source of religious knowledge, the 66 books of Scripture abundantly and fully comprehend all things that are necessary for the Christian life and eternal salvation.

B. Diversity and Unity of the Bible

Diversity of beliefs among Christians in some instances go back to the diversity of Scripture. The formation of the Bible spanned about 1,500 years and was written by some 40 authors. It bears the marks of different cultures and individuals with varying backgrounds, training, language, and styles of writing. By inspiring them to write the Scriptures, the Holy Spirit used the experiences, thought patterns, and tongues of people as diverse as Moses, Jeremiah, Mark, and Paul. *Because of its rich diversity every person who takes the Bible seriously does not come out with the same results.* To illustrate this, some minimize the importance of spiritual gifts for today; but on the basis of the New Testament, Pentecostals see the gifts of the Spirit as vital to the ongoing life and ministry of the church.

Obviously not everything that is presented as Christian has the support of the Scriptures. But a widespread opinion today is that almost anything can be proved by Scripture. However, the Bible itself sets the limits on Christian doctrine. Though diverse in form and content, the Bible is one book. It reveals to us one God and no more. It has one doctrinal system, one standard of morals, and one plan of salvation. The Bible presents views of God from various perspectives, and there are also a number of different ways that doctrines, moral principles, and God's plan of salvation are set forth in Scripture. But none of the teachings of the Bible are contradictory. For example, the Old Testament law prepares us to accept Christ as Savior and Lord. The law of Moses was given to teach us that we are sinners and to lead us to Christ by faith (see Galatians 3:24, 25).

God has progressively revealed His truth. The Bible provides us a record of God's gradual revelation of Himself in the history of the Hebrew people, leading up to the fullness of time when the Son of God came into the world. From Genesis through Revelation the Bible sets forth truth in a consistent manner so that we may know God and learn His will.

C. Authority of the Bible

Pentecostals ardently defend the divine authority of the Scriptures. For Pentecostals the Bible is the final and supreme authority for Christian doctrine and practice. The authority of the Scriptures does not depend on any source other than God. The Scriptures come to us as the divinely inspired Word of God

(2 Timothy 3:16). What they teach is binding on us. *Hence the authority of the Scriptures is founded in God and in truth. Through the Scriptures the Holy Spirit conveys God's message of truth and speaks through them the very Word of God.*

As the supreme authority in all matters of doctrine and practice, the Bible is God's Word. God's Word is truth (John 17:17). God never lies (Titus 1:2) and cannot be charged with making mistakes. The truthfulness of the Bible is compatible with the character of God. God has always been truthful; otherwise He would not be God. To ascribe error to Scripture (as it was originally given) does not do justice to the character of God. A fully reliable and authoritative Bible agrees with what we know about God's character.

Because the Bible comes from God, it carries an authority above "traditions of men" and human reason. *Scripture has universal authority with universal applications. This conviction has prompted Pentecostals to submit to biblical authority in every facet of their faith and religious practice.* The Bible is affirmed as the norm for the life of the church and the personal life of each believer. Every word and experience is to be measured by the teaching of Holy Scripture. The overarching authority of Scripture—a tenet which found renewal in the Reformation—is affirmed by Pentecostals.

D. Contents of the Bible

When we consider the contents of the Bible, we are impressed with the supernatural quality of Scripture. By examining its contents we see that this is no ordinary book. Throughout, God is magnified and declared to be the Creator. Men and women are said to be created in the image of God. The fall and judgment of mankind is recorded. Details of God's provision for our salvation are given. The Bible portrays the consummation of all things at the second coming of Christ.

The Bible is a book of comfort and hope against despair—in a word, it is a book of divine deliverance in which we see the power of God's grace to set sinners free from the bondage of sin. The unity of its message is nothing less than Jesus Christ. *Both the Old and New Testaments find their center in Jesus, the incarnate Son of God and the Savior of the world.* Jesus bore witness that the Scriptures pointed to Himself. To the Jews He said, "You search the Scriptures, for in them you think you have eternal life; and these are they which testify of Me" (John 5:39). On the same occasion, He said, "For if you believed Moses, you would believe Me; for he wrote about Me" (v. 46).

Jesus Christ left no doubt that the Scriptures find their unity in His person. After His resurrection He met two disciples on the road to Emmaus. He said to them, "O foolish ones, and slow of heart to believe in all that the prophets have spoken! Ought not the Christ to have suffered these things and to enter into His glory?" (Luke 24:25, 26). Jesus knew that His ministry was foreshadowed in the Old Testament writings. So "beginning at Moses and all the Prophets, He expounded to them in all the Scriptures the things concerning Himself" (v. 27).

Likewise the sermons recorded in the Book of Acts affirm that Jesus Christ is the center of the Scriptures. At Pentecost, Peter used Psalm 16:8-11 and Psalm 110:1 as texts for the proclamation of the risen Savior (Acts 2:25-36). In a later sermon he identified Jesus as the prophet about whom Moses had spoken in Deuteronomy 18:15, 18, 19 (Acts 3:20-22). When the Ethiopian asked Philip the meaning of Isaiah 53, Philip, "beginning at this Scripture, preached Jesus to him (Acts 8:35). From Psalm 2:7,

Isaiah 55:3, and Psalm 16:10, Paul preached Christ at Antioch of Pisidia (Acts 13:32-37). The preaching of Paul rested on the centrality of Christ throughout the Scriptures. His Christ-centered method was evident in his preaching at Thessalonica in a synagogue. "Paul, as his custom was, went in to them, and for three Sabbaths reasoned with them from the Scriptures, explaining and demonstrating that the Christ had to suffer and rise again from the dead, and saying 'This Jesus whom I preach to you is the Christ'" (Acts 17:2, 3). Throughout Paul's epistles this same appeal is made to Christ as the fulfillment of the Old Testament.

Others also saw Christ as the center of the Scriptures. Apollos, the Alexandrian Jew *boiling with the Spirit* (see Acts 18:25) vigorously refuted the Jews by showing from the prophecies of the Old Testament that Jesus is the Christ (v. 28). Moreover, the same understanding of Scripture appears in the epistles of Peter and John, and in Hebrews, James, and Jude—all affirm that Christ is the unifying center of the Scriptures. The living Christ is the central content of both the Old and New Testaments.

E. Clarity of the Bible

The Bible speaks in clear and definite terms. All the teachings that are laid down in Scripture are accessible to the average reader. Scripture claims to set forth clearly God's Word—"Your word is a lamp to my feet and a light to my path" (Psalm 119:105; cf. v. 130; 19:8). The gospel itself is clear. It is no fault of the gospel that we are unable to discern its glory. The minds of those who do not believe have been blinded by Satan, the god of this age. The veil of blindness is over their hearts and minds, not over the gospel (see 2 Corinthians 4:3, 4). The gospel runs counter to human ways of thinking. This fact explains why individuals may remain unmoved by its proclamation. As the Bible says,

"The message of the cross" becomes to some a stumbling block and sheer foolishness (1 Corinthians 1:18-25).

Of course, a few passages of Scripture are obscure. Peter recognized that some things in Paul's letters are hard to understand (2 Peter 3:16). However, *almost any passage in the Bible can be illuminated by the observations of competent Bible scholars. But the average Christian with limited resources can also understand most of the Bible.* Scripture is open to all. To regard it otherwise would be to maintain that Scripture is incoherent and its meaning open only to those who have the capacity to probe its hidden meanings. Pentecostals take no such approach. They are convinced that the deeper significance of the biblical text is perceived through the eyes of faith. And it is not possible to penetrate to the heart of its message without the help of the Holy Spirit. The apostle Paul affirmed that we need the enlightenment of the Holy Spirit to interpret the Scripture:

> But as it is written: "Eye has not seen, nor ear heard, nor have entered into the heart of man the things which God has prepared for those who love Him." But God has revealed them to us through His Spirit. For the Spirit searches all things, yes, the deep things of God *(1 Corinthians 2:9, 10).*

The Holy Spirit gives the believer in Christ a deeper insight into Scripture. As the Spirit searches even the deep things of God, He illuminates our understanding to the mysteries of the gospel.

F. Influence of the Bible

The Bible has exerted more influence on humankind than any other book. The writings of Confucius, the Koran, and the Book of Mormon have had influence, but not in comparison with the Bible. The Bible is still the most influential book on earth even though it is variously understood or even totally misunderstood by some.

The Bible informs us of the Savior and provides the foundation for the faith and life of the church. *Through the message of the Bible and the power of the Holy Spirit, millions have accepted Christ as their Savior. The Bible especially shapes and guides the Pentecostal community in the practice of faith and in adherence to sound doctrine.* God's Word is concerned with right living, right doctrine, and right relationships between God and His people as well as between all brothers and sisters in His church.

Even beyond the bounds of the church, the Bible has had a strong influence. It has had a significant influence on literature, art, and music (e.g., Tennyson's "Crossing the Bar," Michelangelo's *The Last Supper*, and Handel's *Messiah*). Moreover, the Bible has had an impact on the laws of most nations and has helped to bring recognition of the human rights of slaves, women, and minorities, and the improvement of life for the poor and needy.

Chapter 2

REVELATION
OF
GOD

Revelation is the disclosure or unveiling of something hidden. Without revelation God would remain hidden. This fact is implied by the question "Can a man by searching find out God?" (Job 11:7, free translation). In His goodness and wisdom God has been pleased to reveal Himself and to make His plan of salvation known to us. The reason we know God is that He has revealed Himself. So by the use of the term *revelation,* we mean *communication*—God communicating truth about Himself and about His plan of salvation.

It has become commonplace to describe revelation as God's disclosure of Himself. God is never precisely described as revealing Himself—at least the phrase "God's self-revelation" does not appear in the Bible. But to understand what is stated in Scripture as the self-revelation of God makes excellent sense. God makes Himself known to us, revealing His character, His relations with us, and the good news of salvation. His words and actions are revealing words and acts, for God has through them disclosed Himself and His plan.

Progressive Revelation

Scripture records a progressive revelation. That is, God gradually revealed Himself and His redemptive purpose until the fullness appeared in Christ. Therefore revelation is educational. Children begin with the ABCs and gradually add to their knowledge. Scripture provides the record of God's long and gradual revelation of Himself leading to Christ. Regularly God manifested Himself in the history of the Hebrew people; but when the fullness of time arrived, He brought His Son Jesus Christ into the world. The coming of Christ was a full manifestation of God. In Christ, God was revealed as He had never been revealed before.

Earlier revelation was incomplete; it was filled out later. But what was added did not minimize the importance of earlier revelation. Sometimes the idea of "progressive revelation" has been appealed to as a basis for discrediting parts of the Scripture. Those who take this view see a steady progression from the lower to the higher and from error to truth. But the fact is that the disclosure of truth was adequate at each stage in which God gave it. Though we reject the view that primitive ideas were laid aside for more advanced ones, later revelation often builds upon and fills out the earlier. Consequently, God can be said to have unfolded gradually His revelation, and so doctrine may also be said to have developed throughout the Scriptures.

The practice of sacrifice is prominent in the Old Testament, but such sacrifices were no longer prescribed in the New Testament. The change was not because a more primitive idea of God was superseded by a more advanced one, but because the sacrifice of Christ fulfilled the sacrificial system. The Old Testament sacrifices pointed to Christ and were intended to teach both the dreadful consequences of sin and the way that God had determined to save sinners. Drawing upon the sacrificial language of the Old Testament, John the Baptist was able to declare, "Behold! The Lamb of God who takes away the sin of the world!" (John 1:29; cf. 1 Peter 1:18, 19). In the Old Testament the full revelation of God is not given. Full revelation did not come until the time of Christ. But when Christ came, He bore witness to the value of the earlier revelation. He said, "Do not think that I came to destroy the Law or the Prophets. I did not come to destroy but to fulfill [them]" (Matthew 5:17). The Old Testament provides genuine nourishment for the Christian life, but the New Testament throws even more light on the truths revealed in the Law and the Prophets.

The Bible records an unfolding of God's revelation over many centuries. *For the Christian, particular statements in Scripture must be interpreted in light of the total biblical revelation. Earlier teachings must be explained in light of later teachings.* No doubt, the sacrificial requirements of the Old Testament were true as far as they went and were valid until Christ came, but they are not an expression of God's will for Christians.

General and Special Revelation

We find that Scripture testifies to two kinds of revelation. Traditionally Christians have classified these as "general" and "special" revelation. Both come from God, are supernatural, and complement each other. General revelation is so described for two reasons. First, it is generally known, that is, it is made known to all people. It is not restricted to any particular group or nation. Second, it is general from the viewpoint of being wider in kind. It refers to revelation that occurs in creation and in the human conscience. In contrast, special revelation is the name given to the revelation in the Scriptures. *The Bible is the book of special revelation.* However, a balanced approach requires that we recognize that God has made Himself known in the Scriptures and through His creation. God has used various means to enrich and deepen our understanding of Him and His will.

A. General Revelation

A general knowledge of God's nature is reflected in creation, and a knowledge of His will is written on the human conscience.

1. In Creation

God speaks to us in His entire creation. The created world (nature) is a manifestation of God's glory, power, and perfection. God's revelation in the world impressed the psalmist when he wrote, "The heavens declare the glory of God; and the firmament shows His handiwork" (Psalm 19:1). By day and night the heavens constantly bear witness of God's majesty and power (v. 2). There is no human speech or language in nature (v. 3), but creation gives an eloquent testimony that God is God. In a similar way, the apostle Paul spoke of the knowledge of God that has been made available to mankind in the created universe. Through the things God has made, "His invisible attributes are clearly seen;" that is, "His eternal power and Godhead" (Romans 1:20) are reflected in the wonders of the universe (cf. Job 40:1—42:6). Creation bears witness of the Creator and discloses that the key to its existence can only be truly found in God. The words of Paul at Lystra present the same view. To the people there he explained that "the living God . . . made the heaven, the earth, the sea, and all things that are in them. . . . Nevertheless He did not leave Himself without witness, in that He did good, gave us rain from heaven and fruitful seasons, filling our hearts with food and gladness" (Acts 14:15-17). Consequently the goodness, wisdom, and power of God are evident in creation.

2. In the Human Conscience

God created this world and men along with it. God has left His imprint upon creation in general. But God specifically endowed man with His own image (Genesis 1:26). Thus every person has a spiritual likeness to God. This unique endowment includes a revelation of God's will in each person. Paul observed that men have the moral law of God written upon their hearts (Romans 2:14, 15). Because God's moral law has left its stamp on the human conscience, we are not without moral insight. Conscience condemns us for the wrong we do. Innate moral insight points to a moral God who has endowed mankind with a basic awareness of right and wrong.

Of course, sin may muffle the voice of conscience. As a result, the conscience is not necessarily an adequate guide. Due to the influence of sin, a person's attitude and actions may reflect the values and ways of society and may be contrary to the universal moral law written in the mind. What is insisted on as being right or acceptable in a society may be morally wrong. So the voice of conscience is rejected or, at least, muffled so that it is not properly heard. But for the Christian, the Holy Spirit is the source of a good conscience. The Spirit, along with the Word of God, enables the Christian to discern between good and evil, and right and wrong.

Even though God reveals Himself in creation and His will

in our conscience, the minds of most individuals are blinded to the significance of this revelation. That was the condition of Gentiles in the first century. God was recognizable: the Gentiles saw God's eternal power and perfections in creation. They knew something about the will of God from the law written in their hearts. But they did not acknowledge, honor, and thank Him. Rather, they despised and falsified the truth about God disclosed in the created world (Romans 1:18-23). They were spiritually blind.

3. Limitation of General Revelation

God's revelation in our conscience and in creation is sufficient to leave us without excuse for sin (Romans 1:20; cf. Acts 17:24-31). But it fails to provide knowledge of God necessary for salvation. Spiritual blindness prevents mankind from seeing clearly God's revelation in creation. And even if we could understand it fully, general revelation would still be inadequate. It tells us nothing about the great doctrines of the Christian faith. Nothing is revealed in the created world about the Trinity, Christ's birth, the atoning death and resurrection of the Savior, and heaven and hell. In its eloquent message no place is given to telling of the Holy Spirit and His ministry in conversion, in sanctification, and in equipping God's people with power and spiritual gifts for service. The world around us manifests God's majesty and power, and it enriches our understanding of Him as a God of order. But what we can learn from the natural world about God tells us nothing about His redemptive plan. Christ, not creation, is the only way of salvation (Matthew 11:27; John 14:6).

4. Value of General Revelation

In spite of the fact that general revelation fails to redeem from sin, it does teach something about the nature of God. According to the apostle Paul, the Gentiles saw in creation God's everlasting power and perfection, but they despised the disclosed truth and worshiped the creature rather than the Creator (Romans 1:18-25). In his message on Mars Hill, Paul seized the fact that the people had erected an altar "TO THE UNKNOWN GOD." In the error of their religion he detected a trace of truth and set forth in his proclamation the God who raised Jesus from the dead (Acts 17:22-31). Many of the world's religions, with their insights and perversions, reflect the human response to revelation in the works of creation and the human longing for salvation.

Because of mankind's natural limits and spiritual blindness, the significance of revelation in creation remains obscure (cf. 1 Thessalonians 4:5; 1 Corinthians 1:21). *Only eyes enlightened by faith can have a proper estimate of the truth disclosed in the works of the Creator.* Through the eyes of faith the Christian can clearly see that creation reveals God and he can be led to an appreciation of the world. As Christians we see the things that others see, but by the light of the Holy Spirit we can see them in a different way. The glory of the Creator God is seen by us on the face of Jesus Christ (2 Corinthians 4:6). Divine revelation in creation reached its climax in Christ. Adam was created in the image and likeness of God (Genesis 1:26), but Christ is infinitely more than man. He is the God of creation, for "all things were made through Him, and without Him nothing was made that was made" (John 1:3). Christ was not only the cause of creation, He is also the goal of creation: "All things were created . . . for Him" (Colossians 1:16).

By experiencing the transforming grace of Christ, we can perceive clearly the truth about God in creation. Mere human attempts to understand God's work in creation result in distortions and perversions similar to those of Paul's day (Romans 1:21-32). Only by God's revelation in Christ and by eyes illuminated by the Holy Spirit can we have an appreciation of general revelation worthy of our Creator.

B. Special Revelation

Creation sets before us the majesty and power of God. The moral law in the heart condemns us for sinning, but it offers us no saving knowledge of God. Because of our spiritual condition, we need divine assistance. The Bible meets this need. It is God's special word to us and embodies the record of God's great plan of redemption accomplished in Christ and by the Holy Spirit. The Old and New Testaments are the record of God's deeds and words. A distinguishing mark of the Bible is that it records again and again what "Thus says the Lord" and stresses the fact of revelation.

1. Special Revelation as Historical

To describe revelation as historical involves the claim that God acts in history. God has revealed Himself in particular periods of time and to definite people. In history He became known as the God of Abraham, Isaac, and Jacob. God acted decisively in the events of the Flood, the Exodus, the giving of the Law at Sinai, the Babylonian Captivity, and the death and resurrection of Jesus Christ. The historical character of the message of Jesus must not be overlooked. Stressing this fact, Paul affirmed that Christ died, that He was buried, and that He rose from the dead the third day (1 Corinthians 15:3, 4). Then he went on to say that apart from the fact of Christ's resurrection, preaching the gospel is empty and Christian faith is vain (vv. 14-17).

The opening of Luke's Gospel (1:1-4), which appears to

have in view the contents of the Book of Acts as well as the remainder of the Gospel of Luke, describes the Christian message as "an account of the things that have been fulfilled among us" (v. 1, *NIV*). The message of the gospel is rooted and grounded in historical events that were seen and heard. Special revelation consists of God's decisive acts in history, especially in events such as the death and the resurrection of Christ. Moreover, what God has disclosed directly is embodied in the Holy Scriptures as the very Word of God.

2. Means of Special Revelation

By the study of the Scriptures it becomes clear that God has used a number of means to reveal Himself.

a. *Through providence.* The term *providence* means that God is the ruler of the world. The people of Israel were convinced of God's providential rule. During their captivity in Egypt, God raised up Moses and made him their leader. After they went forth out of Egypt, they believed that God had delivered them. In the wilderness God threatened to destroy them, but Moses' plea brought Israel mercy (Exodus 32:11-14; Deuteronomy 9:26-29). When the people of Israel disobeyed, again and again the prophets explained that the calamities that befell Israel were not mere natural disasters but divine judgments for sin, that is, events of revelation. They saw God's ongoing activity in the world. They interpreted the deliverance of Israel from Egypt as an act of divine mercy and judgment.

Likewise, the fortunes of other people were in the hands of God. God dealt with nations such as Egypt (Exodus 9:13-17) and Assyria (Isaiah 10:12-19). His rule brought the rise and the fall of governments. Divine Providence disclosed that "righteousness exalts a nation, but sin is a reproach to any people" (Proverbs

45

14:34). By His rule God shows His concern for people and His judgment of sin. This form of revelation takes us beyond what creation reveals about the living God. It discloses that God promotes good, judges evil, and cares for the world He created (Job 38; 39; Isaiah 45:12; 48:12, 13; 52:10).

b. *Through miracles.* Through the laws of nature is God's customary way of working. The laws of nature are predictable and conform to the natural order we know. When God acts to supersede the order of nature, a miracle occurs. So we can say that miracles are special providential acts of God. In Scripture they are extraordinary works of God, not designed just to provoke excitement but to reveal God's presence, power, and redemptive plan. Miracles, such as the instantaneous healing of the sick and the raising of the dead, reveal divine judgment and mercy.

The true significance of the miracles of Christ cannot be explained as mere displays of His power but as disclosures of His person and ministry. His first miracle—changing water to wine—manifested His glory (John 2:11). That is, this miraculous sign of changing the water pointed to Christ's deity—that the Son of God had come in the flesh. The raising of Lazarus from the dead found its significance in Jesus' own words: "I am the resurrection and the life" (John 11:25). So this miracle was a revelation of Christ's life-giving power.

c. *Through direct communication and manifestations.* On some occasions God spoke to individuals in an audible voice (Genesis 2:16, 17; 3:8-19; Exodus 19:9; Acts 23:11). There were instances where God revealed His presence in nature, such as by columns of smoke (Genesis 15:17) and the whirlwind (Job 38:1; 40:6). God "appeared" to Abraham in Mamre (Genesis 18:1) and to Moses in the burning bush (Exodus 3:2). The "Angel of the LORD" occupies a prominent place in Old Testament manifestations of God (Genesis 16:7-14; 22:11-18; Exodus 3:2). Dreams and visions were a common means of revelation (Numbers 12:6; Joel 2:28; Amos 7-9). Dreams occurred during sleep, but a vision was normally perceived with "eyes wide open." Frequently those who saw visions heard a word from God that clarified the meaning of a particular appearance (Isaiah 6:8; Ezekiel 2:1-4; Jeremiah 1:11-14).

The revelations given to the prophets involved the witness of the Spirit in their hearts. In the New Testament the Spirit is described as the Spirit of revelation and illumination (Mark 13:11; Luke 12:12; John 14:17; Acts 6:10). As a result of the outpouring of the Spirit, God communicates with His Spirit-filled people through visions, dreams, and the prophetic proclamation of the Word (Acts 2:17). In a number of ways God communicates directly with His people.

d. *Through Christ.* Revelation reached its culmination in Jesus Christ. In the past God spoke "at various times and in different ways" by the Old Testament prophets but "has in these last days spoken . . . by His Son" (Hebrews 1:1, 2). Revelation before Christ had as its goal His person and ministry. His unique role in revelation emerges clearly in John's Gospel. "No one has seen God at any time. The only begotten Son, who is in the bosom of the Father, He has declared Him" (1:18). With the coming of Christ into the world, revelation took a personal form. It was no longer merely a matter of discerning God's activity in nature and history. Jesus of Nazareth was God in the flesh.

In Jesus, the glory of God, the divine presence, was seen on earth. His deeds brought true and definitive knowledge of God. What He did as well as what He said revealed God. According to John 14:10, His actions and words are set forth on the same level: "The words that I speak . . . I do not speak on My own authority; but the Father who dwells in Me does the works." His miracles of healing the sick disclosed that the kingdom of God had come (Luke 11:20). His message consisted of what He heard from the Father (John 8:26). Jesus' actions and words revealed the character of God. That is, Christ revealed God's love, power, grace, and righteousness.

Christ came to bear witness to the truth. He was more than a teacher of the truth. The Old Testament prophets introduced their messages with the words "Thus says the Lord." Jesus could declare that He was not only a bringer of the truth but also the truth itself. He embodied in His person the fullness of God's truth so that He could say, "I am the truth" (see John 14:6). He was the supreme manifestation and the unique mediator (communicator) of revelation. The divine Word became flesh and dwelt among us (John 1:14). Manifested in the flesh, Christ was the climax of the Old Testament and the fulfillment of the prophetic promises. As the early Christians believed, He was the Word of God, the supreme revelation of God. He established and disclosed a new and eternal covenant between God and His people. And as Christians, we wait for the glorious revealing of our Lord Jesus Christ on the day of His final coming (1 Corinthians 1:7).

e. *Through the Bible.* The Bible includes all the other means of God's revealing Himself. The prophets and others who were inspired by the Spirit recognized the revelation of God in nature and saw history as the arena of divine activity. And the writers of the New Testament discerned the revelation of God in the life and ministry of Jesus. The significance of Jesus would be unknown to us had it not been for their inspired recognition of Him. From time to time Jesus observed that the prophets had foretold His coming. So His life on earth was to be understood

48

in light of their message (Luke 18:31; 24:27, 44).

His disciples drew attention to the same point. They recognized that Jesus' significance rested on the fact that He was the fulfillment of the Old Testament prophecies. But even more so, they were able to look on His earthly life in the light of His cross and resurrection. So they saw the significance of His life in a way they had not earlier. By knowledge of His ministry and through the Holy Spirit, they were able to interpret the events of His life on the earth. So what we find is that revelation took place not only in the events of Jesus' life but also in the interpretation of those events by the biblical writers. To state it another way, the revelation of God is realized by both events and words. The words of the biblical writers proclaim the significance of the events and clarify the mystery contained in them. Therefore the Bible is both the inspired record of the events and the inspired interpretation of their significance woven into one account. It is holy history, for the Bible is the record of God's deeds in history and of their significance. Because of this the Bible embodies God's revelation to us.

The Holy Spirit and the Continuance of Revelation

To have seen Jesus was to have seen the Father (John 14:9). His whole life and work on the earth manifested God. Through His words He proclaimed God. By His signs and wonders He demonstrated the presence of God. The role of Christ as revealer reached its climax when He ascended into heaven. *It is now the function of the Holy Spirit to extend to us the revelation that the Lord brought and to bring about a deeper understanding of it.*

The Holy Spirit continually makes accessible the revelation of God in Christ. Jesus promised His followers that the Holy Spirit "will teach you . . . and bring to your remembrance all things that I said to you" (John 14:26). This was not a promise made to the apostles alone. The Spirit, who spoke by the prophets and by the apostles, dwells in all believers for the purpose of guiding them into the truth. Only by the Spirit of truth can we genuinely know and identify Jesus as Lord: "No one can say that Jesus is Lord except by the Holy Spirit" (1 Corinthians 12:3).

By the Spirit the eyes of our minds are opened so we can see God's revelation in Christ (2:14). Paul affirmed that God revealed His Son to him (Galatians 1:11-16). And then he explained that this revelation came about in that "God has sent forth the Spirit of His Son into our hearts, crying out, 'Abba, Father!'" (4:6). At Pentecost, Peter, enlightened and empowered by the Holy Spirit, proclaimed the significance of God's revelation in the death and resurrection of Christ (Acts 2:14-41). The Spirit reveals afresh the significance of the biblical message so that all generations may participate in the saving benefits of Christ.

Truth revealed to us by the Holy Spirit conforms in all essentials to the message of the prophets and apostles. So the modern reader of Scripture requires the same assistance of the Spirit as did the biblical authors. Only by the help of the Holy Spirit can the heart of the biblical message be penetrated. In accord with true Pentecostal conviction, revelation becomes real to generation after generation by the Holy Spirit. As we are enlightened by the Spirit, we see things that others see, but with an extra dimension. The Spirit makes revelation live for us. It is well for us to remember that what does not agree with the Scriptures has no valid claim to the term *revelation. The Holy Spirit leads us to the Scriptures. There are no "new revelations" that render us no longer dependent on the Scriptures.*

Chapter 3

INSPIRATION
OF THE
SCRIPTURES

The Bible is the voice of God speaking to mankind across the centuries. Convinced of this fact, Pentecostals have viewed the Bible as the primary witness of God. That is, the message of God was recorded in the biblical text by men inspired by the Holy Spirit. The fact that the Scriptures were inspired by the Holy Spirit makes them unique. Holy men wrote as the Spirit moved them, but the human authors had an active part in the composition of Scripture. The Bible bears the marks of divine inspiration, and it also bears the marks of different human personalities who contributed to its composition.

From the time Jesus Christ came into the world, He was both fully divine and fully human; the same is true of the Bible. The Bible is entirely the Word of God and at the same time entirely the word of men in that they wrote it. Early Pentecostals regarded the writers of Scripture as mere pens in the hands of the Holy Spirit. In time, this view of inspiration proved to be inadequate. As Pentecostal believers now recognize, the inspired writers were not merely passive instruments in the hands of God. They were real authors, because in many cases they recorded their personal experiences and each wrote in his own style.

The Term *Inspiration*

Revelation is what God has said and done. It makes truth known. But inspiration guarantees and preserves truth. The view that the Bible is the inspired Word of God expresses a firm confidence that revelation given in Scripture is true and that the Bible cannot be treated as just another human document. "All Scripture is given by [the] inspiration of God" (2 Timothy 3:16). The words "given by [the] inspiration of God" are the translation of the Greek word *theopneustos*, literally meaning "God-breathed" or "inspired of God." This term indicates *how* the Scriptures came to be. Scripture is the result of the creative breath or Spirit of God. *Divine breath* in the Old Testament often meant the creative activity of the Holy Spirit. So we read, "The Spirit of God has made me, and the breath of the Almighty gives me life" (Job 33:4). The Scripture is a product of the creative work of the Holy Spirit. Although men wrote it, the Holy Spirit determined the content and character of the Scripture. The distinctive hallmark of Scripture is that it owes its origin to the creative activity of the Holy Spirit.

As we can conclude from our discussion to this point, inspiration is not in accordance with popular usage. It may be said that Shakespeare was inspired to write or that the reading of Scripture is inspirational. However, the inspiration of Scripture is quite different from these and makes the Bible different from all other books. *The Bible has a superior quality that sets it apart from other literature. It cannot be viewed as the work of literary geniuses. It is God-breathed and has a divine quality that makes it fully reliable for faith and practice.*

The Mystery of Inspiration

We are not told in Scripture exactly how the writers experienced the inspiration of the Holy Spirit. But we must not forget that holy men wrote as they were *moved* by the Holy Spirit (2 Peter 1:21). The Bible is the work of men to whom the Word of God was revealed. This fact does not detract from its divine origin and authority. The Holy Spirit accommodated Himself to the thought patterns of people as diverse as Moses, Isaiah, Mark, and Paul.

To regard the Bible as both divine and human has a parallel in Jesus Christ. He came into the world as a man, but at the same time He was the unique Son of God. Nobody has been able to explain to our complete satisfaction the union of the divine and the human in the person of Jesus. And just as the union of the divine and the human in the incarnate Christ remains a profound mystery, so does the relation of the divine and the human in the Scriptures. God has expressed His Word through the words of men. Yet the aspects of divine and human in the writing of the Scripture must also be viewed by us as a profound mystery. George Florovsky states it so well:

> The Scriptures are "inspired," they are the Word of God. What is the inspiration can never be properly defined— there is mystery therein. It is a mystery of the divine- human encounter. We cannot fully understand in what manner "God's holy men" heard the Word of their Lord and how they could articulate it in the words of their own dialect. Yet, even in their human transmission, it was the voice of God (*Creation and Redemption*, p. 27.)

Witnesses to Inspiration

A. The Witness of God

An appeal can be made to no greater authority than God. God himself bears witness to the truth of the Bible. By the ministry of the Holy Spirit a person is brought to believe the truth of Scripture, and thus to believe in Jesus Christ. The Bible tells how we can be saved and live the Christian life. It teaches that God is triune—Father, Son, and Holy Spirit. It tells that the gifts of the Spirit are vital to the ministry of the church. And these truths are confirmed by God in the experiences of His people.

The people of God have experienced the indwelling Holy Spirit as a witness in their hearts that the Bible is the Word of God. The Holy Spirit enlightens the heart and intellect to the truth of Scripture and assures believers that all Scripture is inspired of God. Although this witness of the Spirit is in the hearts of the believers, in their lives the truths of Scripture are a reality. By the continuing witness of the Holy Spirit, God attests the supreme authority and trustworthiness of the Bible. Thus God makes Himself the guarantor of the truthfulness and reliability of His own Word.

B. The Witness of Scripture

In the Bible there are statements that clearly affirm Scripture to be the inspired Word of God. Just as a witness in a court of law is allowed to engage in self-testimony, the claims of the Bible are admissible evidence for divine inspiration.

In the Old Testament, it is clear that God spoke through His servants. Before the advent of Christ, God spoke at various times and in different ways by the prophets to His people (Hebrews 1:1). On a number of occasions, Moses reminded the people of Israel that his message was given by divine authority. David claimed divine inspiration by saying, "The Spirit of the Lord spoke by me, and His word was on my tongue" (2 Samuel 23:2). Frequently prophets like Jeremiah, Ezekiel, and Isaiah prefaced their message with such words as "Thus says the Lord," "The word of the Lord came to me, saying," or "The Lord said to me."

54

Christ himself affirmed the Old Testament as the inspired Word of God. He asked, "Why do you . . . transgress the commandment of God because of your tradition?" (Matthew 15:3). By implication Jesus suggested that the commandment (the Old Testament) was the Word of God. Transgression of the commandment made the Jews guilty of undermining the authority of God. Moreover, to introduce citations from the Old Testament, Jesus frequently used the expression "It is written." This expression was used by the Jews to indicate that a quotation came from one of the sacred books and therefore a divinely inspired book. Christ emphasized that He did not come to destroy the Law and the Prophets but to fulfill them, and that not one jot or dot of Scripture would pass away until all things in it are accomplished (Matthew 5:17, 18). He announced that heaven and earth would pass away but that His words would not pass away (Matthew 24:35). He also asserted that Scripture is the Word of God and cannot be broken (John 10:35).

The apostles affirmed the same view of the Old Testament. According to Paul, all Scripture is given by the inspiration of God (2 Timothy 3:16). Peter asserted that the ancient prophets "spoke as they were moved by the Holy Spirit" (2 Peter 1:21). The prophets were men to whom the Word of God came. God said to Jeremiah, "Behold, I have put My words in your mouth" (1:9); and to Ezekiel, "You shall speak My words to them" (2:7). Such men were spokesmen of the Holy Spirit. Before the outpouring of the Spirit at Pentecost, Peter appealed to the passage in Psalm 69:25, "which the Holy Spirit spoke before by the mouth of David concerning Judas" (Acts 1:16, 20). Likewise, Zacharias recalled that God "spoke by the mouth of His holy prophets" (Luke 1:70). According to the testimony of Scripture, the words of the prophets expressed the very Word of God.

Inspiration also extends to the New Testament. Jesus promised that the Holy Spirit would guide the apostles into all truth (John

16:13). For as Christ said, "He will take of what is Mine and declare it to you" (v. 14). Later, Paul confirmed this by declaring that his insight and words were given by the Holy Spirit. For this reason he said the Spirit had revealed the deep truths of God. But he added that the Spirit also provides the language necessary to communicate divine truth. "These things we . . . speak, not in words which man's wisdom teaches but which the Holy Spirit teaches" (see 1 Corinthians 2:9-13). So Paul spoke of his words as Spirit-taught and claimed that Christ was speaking in him (2 Corinthians 13:3).

At an early time, Paul's letters were regarded as Scripture. Speaking of Paul's writings as being difficult to understand, Peter said, "Those who are untaught and unstable twist to their own destruction, as they do also the rest of the Scriptures" (2 Peter 3:16). These words place the Pauline Epistles on a par with "the rest of the Scriptures," that is, with the Old Testament. Since they were classed with the Old Testament, we have a definite testimony to the divine inspiration of Paul's writings.

When the church accepted the 66 books of the Bible as Scripture, that strongly affirmed the Christian conviction that the entire Old and New Testaments are inspired by the Holy Spirit. The Scriptures are obviously supernatural and cannot be reduced to the level of ordinary human documents. In a unique sense they are God's Word because they are fully inspired and embody for us the unchanging Word of God.

Full Inspiration and Reliability of the Bible

The Bible as a whole is the inspired Word of God. By implication, this statement affirms it to be a reliable revelation of God. The term that has been customarily used to describe this characteristic of the Bible is infallibility. To say the Bible is infallible is to mean that it is completely reliable and does not lead people astray. It states the exact truths that the Holy Spirit intended to convey. The writing of the Scriptures by the prophets and apostles does not in any way detract from the divine origin and authority of the Bible. Full inspiration means the Holy Spirit guided the writers not only in their ideas but also in the selection of their words. God joined His Word with the words of men in the Scriptures. So the Bible is fully reliable because of the Divine Author within and behind the human authors.

A. The Original Autographs

Conservative Christians speak of the Bible as the infallible Word of God, but they have felt it necessary to qualify this conviction. *That is, the original manuscripts (original autographs) were infallible as they came from the hands of the authors. But none of the manuscripts which bore the actual signatures of the authors have been preserved. The existing manuscripts are copies of copies.* The printing press, as we all know, is relatively modern. Before the modern means of printing was available, people copied the Scriptures by hand. The original manuscripts of the writers of Scripture wore out from use and age. So it became necessary that copies be made to preserve their works. Naturally when a document of any length is copied by hand, the copyist may alter the text unintentionally in a few places. As scribes copied and recopied the Scriptures, there was the possibility for differences in wording to develop over the years. Such differences did develop, but most of them were very minor.

All the currently existing manuscripts of the Hebrew Old Testament and of the Greek New Testament are copies. Prior to 1947 the oldest known manuscript of the Old Testament had been copied in the ninth century A.D. But the discovery of the Dead Sea Scrolls provided manuscripts of the Old Testament dating to a little before the first advent of Christ. Then there are many hundreds of New Testament manuscripts. These are either parts of the Greek New Testament or the entire Greek New Testament. But among the many manuscripts there is not a single autograph, not a single original copy of any book of the New Testament. However, some of the copies are only once or twice removed from the original autographs, while others are many times removed. But a comparison of any two lengthy texts preserved from the earliest centuries reveals that they are not identical. The same applies to the Hebrew Old Testament.

In view of the differences in the existing manuscripts, there is wisdom in speaking of the Scriptures as infallible in the original autographs or as originally given to the prophets and apostles. Due to these differences an entire branch of biblical studies, known as textual criticism, is devoted to determining the most reliable biblical text. Although the original autographs are extinct, the goal of textual criticism is to determine as nearly as possible what those autographs were. Without question this goal has been accomplished, and we have a reliable text of both the Old and the New Testament. None of the variant readings in the manuscripts raise questions regarding any cardinal doctrine or teaching of the Christian faith. *God by His grace preserved His written Word as it was transmitted from generation to generation.* God's providential care extends to His written Word. By divine providence the Word of God has been preserved.

B. The Ideas and Words of Scripture

Inspiration applies to both the ideas and the words of Scripture. Scripture makes no distinction between the inspiration of the sacred writers' ideas and the inspiration of their words. The words, required to express the ideas, were inspired by the Spirit. "Holy men of God spoke as they were moved by the Holy Spirit" (2 Peter 1:21; cf. 2 Timothy 3:16). The Greek word for *moved* (*pheromenoi*) means "carried along" or "borne along." *Due to the direct influence of the Holy Spirit, the writers' choice of words expressed the truth God intended to convey. This is what we mean by "verbal" or "plenary" inspiration of Scripture.*

Some have assumed that verbal inspiration made the biblical writers passive instruments, robbing them of their individuality. The Spirit did not inspire Scripture that way. Rather He used the various abilities of the writers and their particular styles of writing to produce the Bible. *The writers of Scripture were not like a typewriter that is completely passive when used. They wrote, but God so guided and directed them in their writing that their words are the message of the Holy Spirit (see Mark 12:36; Acts 1:16; Hebrews 3:7; 10:15).*

As has been noted, the relation of the divine and the human in the writing of Scripture is a profound mystery. However, inspiration includes the Spirit's dealing directly with the writers and the writers' responding to Him obediently and faithfully so that they set forth the truth in just the right way.

C. Trustworthiness of Scripture

The trustworthiness of the Scripture rests on the fact that it is the inspired Word of God. Scripture can truly be regarded as "the faithful word" (see Titus 1:9) and "worthy of all acceptance" (see 1 Timothy 1:15). It merits our trust because Scripture sets forth the truth. However, this is not to deny that it is difficult to harmonize some statements in Scripture with other statements. *Nevertheless, the reliability of Scripture does not depend on our resourcefulness to prove its truthfulness at every point. The accuracy of Scripture is not sacrificed if we acknowledge that we may not have the solution to a particular difficulty.* This is a wiser course of action than an artificial harmonization, which by the stretch of the imagination seems hardly valid. So the reliability of Scripture is not placed in jeopardy by admitting that presently we do not have sufficient information to give convincing answers in some cases.

Still, we should be aware that a number of once-puzzling features of Scripture have now been resolved. Biblical archaeology has done a remarkable job of confirming the historical accuracy of the biblical narratives. As archaeologists continue their work, it is likely that fresh discoveries will provide more supporting evidence and will throw yet more light on the nature of things as they were in Bible times.

We should also understand that many of the alleged problems in Scriptures are due to our failure to interpret them correctly. The Scriptures should be interpreted the way the prophets and apostles intended them to be understood. In the Bible some statements are in poetic or symbolic language and should not be taken in a literal sense. As an example, take Jesus' words when He instituted the Lord's Supper. He took the bread, saying, "Take, eat; this is My body," and then the cup and said, "This is My blood" (Matthew 26:26-28). Obviously Jesus did not hold His body and blood in His own hands. The bread symbolized the body of Christ that was broken for us, and the cup the blood that He poured out on the cross. Some truths can only be stated in a figurative way. But it is easy for us who are of a literal turn of mind to forget that Scripture at times employs figurative language.

Some questions of interpretation may remain unresolved, but the teachings of Scripture have repeatedly proven themselves to be true. No one would argue that the doctrines of the Trinity, the Incarnation, and the Atonement rest on our ability to explain these mysteries. Neither does the inspiration and reliability of Scripture depend on our ability to provide a logical explanation for every difficulty in Scripture we encounter.

Chapter 4

CANONICITY
OF THE
SCRIPTURES

The study of the canonicity of Holy Scripture discloses the uniqueness and superiority of the Bible. Such a study focuses on how the Scriptures came to be as they now exist. As we examine how the Bible became the Bible, it becomes clear that it is more than a collection of great books. *Before the books of the Bible were recognized by the church as authoritative Scripture, they already had authority.* The church simply acknowledged those books as being Scripture that were already widely accepted as Holy Scripture. However, the thing that makes a book canonical is not merely its acceptance, but what the Holy Spirit did in causing it to be written with authority. The church can do no more than recognize what the Spirit has done. If a book is inspired by the Spirit, then it is canonical. As a product of the Holy Spirit, it belongs to the Canon.

The Term *Canon*

The word *canon* is derived from the Greek *kanon*, which originally meant "a staff" or "measuring rod." In pre-Christian times it referred to a norm or standard by which something is evaluated. The term was used this way in the New Testament (see in Greek 2 Corinthians 10:13, 15, 16; Galatians 6:16). By the second century, Christians understood that *canon* stood for the books that were the authoritative source and rule for doctrine and practice. *The canon of Scripture consists of all the books of the Old and New Testaments recognized as the Word of God because they are uniquely inspired of God.*

Forming the Canon was a gradual and long process. Specific books achieved recognition as they were widely used over an extended period of time in the worship and life of the church. Two groups of books make up our Canon: the Old Testament and the New Testament.

The Canon of the Old Testament

From the very beginning the Christian church had a Canon. That Canon consisted of the 39 books of the Old Testament. These books were generally accepted during New Testament times as they stand now in our Bible. So *the Canon accepted by the Jews in the first century was identical with the Old Testament Canon accepted by Protestants.* It remains unknown exactly when the Old Testament Canon was fixed, but the process was gradual. There is no reason for us to doubt that the selection was made on the merits of each book and was based on the best spiritual judgment at the time.

A. Three Stages of Development

The canonization of the Old Testament seems traceable to

three stages that correspond to three broad divisions of the Hebrew Old Testament.

1. The Law (Torah)

This division consists of the first five books of the Old Testament: Genesis, Exodus, Leviticus, Numbers, and Deuteronomy. These books, commonly known as the Pentateuch (five rolls), were recognized as having canonical status by the fourth century B.C. Ezra read to the people of Judah from the Book of the Law. This book had been brought from Babylonian Exile to Jerusalem (Nehemiah 8).

When the Samaritans separated from the main body of Judaism, they possessed a version of these books (the Samaritan Pentateuch) and accepted only these as Scripture. The date of the Samaritan schism is generally believed to have occurred early in the first part of the fourth century B.C. But considerably earlier than this, the first five books of the Old Testament were accepted as authoritative Scripture.

The recognition of the first five books as canonical had been anticipated by Josiah (622 or 621 B.C.). "The Book of the Law" (thought to be Deuteronomy 12—26) served as a basis for Josiah's religious reforms throughout his kingdom (2 Kings 22; 23). At a public assembly in Jerusalem, Josiah read the Law and pledged his own obedience to the Lord, and then the people joined with him in support of God's written Law (2 Kings 23:1-3). This reading of the Law must have assisted the Pentateuch toward the early recognition of its canonical status.

Throughout the history of Israel, the Pentateuch (also called the Law) was recognized as having divine authority. When the Law was completed, it became for the devout in Israel the rule for faith and practice. The priests were commanded to read the Law to the people:

"You shall read this law before all Israel in their hearing" (Deuteronomy 31:11). Joshua was told to guide the people in the light of the Law: "This Book of the Law shall not depart from your mouth, but you shall meditate in it day and night, that you may observe to do according to all that is written in it" (Joshua 1:8). The writings of prophets make frequent references to the Law (see Jeremiah 2:8; Hosea 4:6).

To think of Israel without the Law is very difficult. For Israel the Law was binding. It demanded obedience to its commands and prohibitions. Dating back to the time of Moses, Israel regarded the Law as sacred Scripture.

2. The Prophets (Nebiim)

The writings of the prophets comprise the second division of the Old Testament. In addition to the Law, these writings were also regarded as God's Word. The prophets themselves understood that they spoke the Word of God. It was not uncommon for them to assert that they declared the word of the Lord (Isaiah 8:5; Jeremiah 3:6; 13:1; Ezekiel 21:1; Amos 3:1). According to their own testimony, the message they proclaimed was not their own creation but the message of God.

Hebrew tradition divides the writings of the prophets into two groups—the Former and the Latter Prophets. The books of the Former Prophets are Joshua, Judges, 1 and 2 Samuel, and 1 and 2 Kings. The books of the Latter Prophets are Isaiah, Jeremiah, Ezekiel, and the 12 Minor Prophets. It may seem strange to classify Joshua, Judges, Samuel, and Kings as prophetical books. These are historical books, records of the experiences of Israel from the time of settlement in Canaan to the fall of Jerusalem in 587 B.C. But they are considered prophetical because they tell of the ministry of prophets like Samuel,

Nathan, Gad, Micaiah, Elijah, and Elisha.

The Old Testament does not tell how the Latter or Former Prophets came to be included in the Canon, but the recognition of the canonical status of these books was natural. The prophets received divine revelation, and the words they uttered were the inspired Word of God. A number of the prophets committed their words to writing. Isaiah commanded that his words be preserved: "Bind up the testimony, seal the law among my disciples" (8:16). Ezekiel knew and quoted words which God had spoken by His former prophets (38:17). *Since the messages of the prophets were inspired and authoritative, it was quite natural for the people of Israel to preserve the written words of the prophets.*

However, not all the prophets committed their messages to writing. The Former Prophets contains accounts of the prophetic ministry of men like Samuel and Elijah, but collections of their messages have not been preserved. Nevertheless, like the Latter Prophets, they were uncompromising spokesmen for God. What is known about the ministry of the Former Prophets indicates they had perfect harmony with the message and ministry of the Latter Prophets. The canonicity of the books of the Former Prophets has not been disputed. The truths set forth in the Former and Latter Prophets demanded of Israel the same obedience to the Law of the Lord. Doubtlessly these books were inspired by the Holy Spirit and are part of the authoritative Word of God.

3. The Writings (Kethubim)

The third division of the Old Testament is the *Writings* or, in Greek, the *Hagiographa* (Holy Writings). Scripture gives no idea who collected these books nor when they were recognized as part of the Canon. The Writings consist of the Psalms, Proverbs,

Job, Daniel, 1 and 2 Chronicles, Ezra, Nehemiah, and the Five Rolls (the Song of Solomon, Ruth, Lamentations, Ecclesiastes, and Esther). The authors of these books were acknowledged to be inspired by the Spirit; but as far as we know, they were not officially recognized as prophets of Israel. Men like David and Daniel exercised the gift of prophecy; but they were not prophets in the official sense of the word. The prophets served as mediators between God and the nation of Israel, announcing the Word of God to the people (Exodus 4:15, 16; 7:1; Deuteronomy 18:18; Jeremiah 1:17). David and Daniel served as statesmen. Thus, as it is in the Hebrew Bible, the Psalms (of David and of others) and the Book of Daniel are rightly placed in the third division of the Old Testament.

The Law and Prophets were understood to have been written by men who belonged to the prophetic order. The third division, the Writings, were not ascribed to the prophets, but they came to be regarded as part of the inspired Word of God. The earliest evidence that we have for the recognition of canonical status of the Writings is an apocryphal work, Ecclesiasticus, written by Jesus ben Sarach. About 132 B.C., the grandson of ben Sarach wrote a prologue to the Greek translation of his grandfather's book. There he spoke about his grandfather's study of the Law and Prophets and of "the other books of our fathers"—a reference to the third division, namely, the Writings. It is likely, therefore, these books were regarded as Holy Scripture prior to the second century B.C.

The Canon of the New Testament

At its beginning the New Testament church possessed a Canon of authoritative writings—the Jewish Scriptures known to us as the Old Testament. As the years passed, the church recognized the inherent authority of another collection of books, the New Testament. This new Canon took its place alongside the Old Testament and consists of 27 books, which appear in the Bible, beginning with the Gospel of Matthew and ending with the Book of Revelation. *The forming of the New Testament resulted from the church's gradual recognition of the canonical status of its 27 books.* Let us look at this process in apostolic and postapostolic times.

A. The Period of the Apostles

A few years after the death and resurrection of Jesus, Christian writings began to flourish. Luke said that many before him had drawn up an account of the Gospel events (Luke 1:1). Many Gospels were written, such as the Gospels According to Thomas, Matthias, and Bartholomew. A number of books of Acts appeared—the Acts of Thomas, the Acts of Andrew, and the Acts of Paul and Thecla. The mass of literature that developed raised questions. What should be accepted as canonical status and distinct from ordinary literature?

Such questions could not be answered satisfactorily without the help of the Holy Spirit. The early church was characteristically a Pentecostal church, a church of the Spirit. Among the early Christians were prophets, apostles, and teachers. These were people of the Spirit and deeply conscious of acting under the guidance of the Holy Spirit. When the decision was made at the Jerusalem Council, it was announced in these words: "It seemed good to the Holy Spirit, and to us" (Acts 15:28). As members of the council, the believers were instruments of the Holy Spirit. Likewise, on different occasions Paul decided a matter confidently, appealing to the fact that he had the Spirit of God (1 Corinthians 7:40). Through the Spirit, Paul consciously claimed authority for his writings: "If anyone does not obey our word in this epistle . . . do not keep company with him" (2 Thessalonians 3:14). He also declared that his preaching was not "the word of men" but "the word of God" (1 Thessalonians 2:13) and that what he spoke was not the words of man's wisdom, but wisdom taught by the Spirit (1 Corinthians 2:13). Paul's claims were in accord with Jesus' promise of the Holy Spirit (John 14:26).

In the time of the apostles, a number of the New Testament books were already recognized as Scripture. The best example of this fact is 2 Peter 3:15, 16, which refers to Paul's letters as Scripture. Paul in 1 Timothy 5:18 quoted Luke 10:7 as Scripture and ascribes to it the same authority as the Old Testament. Jude 17, 18 quotes 2 Peter 3:2 as words spoken by the apostles. From this it is clear that the New Testament confirms that the words of the apostles had authority equal to that of the Old Testament.

B. The Postapostolic Period

From the writings of the early church fathers and other sources can be gleaned information that confirms the canonical authority of the New Testament. Among well-known witnesses of the acceptance of New Testament books as canonical were men such as Clement of Rome, Ignatius, and Irenaeus. Writing to the Corinthian church (about A.D. 95), Clement quoted from 1 Corinthians and clearly used Matthew, John, Romans, Ephesians, James, and possibly 1 Timothy and Titus. Ignatius served as bishop in Antioch about the end of the first century. As he was being carried to Rome to be put to death (martyred in A.D. 107 or 116), he wrote to seven different churches. In these letters it is evident that he knew our New Testament in general. He quoted from Matthew, 1 and 2 Corinthians, and Ephesians and used the phraseology of Luke, John, and a number of Paul's epistles. Ignatius and Clement together bore witness to a large portion of the present New Testament.

The witness of Irenaeus is also significant. He was born in Asia Minor about A.D. 130, became an important figure in France, and served as bishop of the church in Lyons, Gaul. The scope of the New Testament Canon for Irenaeus is quite plain. He quoted extensively from the New Testament and summarized the teachings of the four Gospels. From the apostolic epistles he argued against false doctrines of his time. *In fact, Irenaeus cited most of the New Testament, referring to it as the Scripture, verbally inspired by the Holy Spirit and absolutely true.*

Adding strength to the testimony of Irenaeus is the Muratorian Canon. This list of New Testament Scriptures was composed about A.D. 170. The list includes nearly all our present New Testament books and is part of a manuscript written in the seventh or eighth century. The first lines of the manuscript are missing, but it begins by referring to the third Gospel. Therefore, this description of Luke's Gospel implies that Matthew and Mark were also part of the list. All the books of the New Testament are included except Hebrews, James, and 1 and 2 Peter. But the books that do not appear in the Muratorian Canon were attested by Irenaeus. So this list essentially agrees with Irenaeus, and the two together identify the 27 books of the New Testament exactly.

For all intents and purposes the New Testament Canon was fixed in the second century. At this early time the New Testament was accepted as the Word of God. However, the complete single listing of New Testament books, agreeing exactly with the Bible today, appeared no earlier than A.D. 367 in the "Easter Letter of Athanasius."

Tests of Worthiness

As the early Christians came to grips with what should be accepted as the New Testament Canon, they applied certain tests to determine the worthiness of the books. *Three tests enabled the church to ascertain more exactly what books were authoritative for faith and practice.*

A. Content

Any book which came with the claim to be authoritative was judged by its content. *This test was whether a writing conformed to the orthodox body of Christian doctrine (see 1 Corinthians 11:2; 15:2; 2 Thessalonians 2:15).* If it failed to agree with the truth revealed in Christ, the book was deemed to lack spiritual quality and was not worthy to be included in the Canon. Many of the apocryphal books were rejected for this reason. For example, the Gospel According to Hebrews says the Holy Spirit led Jesus into the desert by picking Him up by the hair of His head. Another apocryphal work, Acts of John, describes Christ as walking on soft sand and leaving no footprints (ch. 93). According to this, Christ appeared to be a man, but He was not a real man of flesh and blood. Such a doctrine was clearly contrary to the biblical teaching that the Son of God "became flesh" (John 1:14). These books and others promoted fictions, extravagances, and even heresies. Because they failed to meet the test of truthfulness and spiritual quality and dignity of authoritative Scripture, they were rejected.

B. Apostolicity

A second test was applied to determine whether a writing deserved to belong in the New Testament Canon: *Was a given book written or backed by an apostle?* Christ had given the apostles commandments through the Spirit (Acts 1:2) and endowed them at Pentecost with the power of the Spirit (2:1-4). The Spirit was to teach them all things, recall to their minds what Jesus had said, and guide them into the fullness of truth (John 14:26; 15:26; 16:13-15). The authority of the apostles was not human but divine, inasmuch as it was derived from Christ. Divine authority was vested also in their writings. They were Jesus' chosen representatives, eyewitnesses to the Gospel events, and the primary interpreters of Jesus' life and ministry.

The church was right when it made apostolicity a basic test, but the Gospels of Mark and Luke and the Book of Acts were not written by an apostle. Still these books were considered to have apostolic authority because they were written by close associates of an apostle. Because Mark was a comrade of Peter's and Luke of Paul's, their writings were deemed to be vested with apostolic authority.

C. Universality

Before a book could be recognized as canonical, another test was applied: *Was it widely accepted as useful for Christian doctrine and living?* A book that had been used throughout the church over a long period of time was in a much better position than a book that had been used by only a few churches and that only recently. Most of the 27 books of the New Testament were universally acknowledged and accepted, but a few were in question—Hebrews, Jude, 2 Peter, 2 and 3 John, James, and the Book of Revelation. However, gradually these too came to be universally accepted.

Divine Providence and the Canon of Scripture

The 66 books which make up the Bible were divinely

brought together. The Scriptures of both the Old and New Testaments are divinely inspired, for holy men of God spoke and wrote them as they were inspired by the Spirit. The story of the formation of the Canon affirms the supreme greatness of the Scriptures. No book can compare with the Bible. It is God's own Word and nothing could stop the 66 books from becoming our Scriptures. God was behind the whole process of the production, collection, and preservation of the Scriptures. By His providence, God gave His Word and enabled His people to recognize and receive it.

Although human factors were evident in the divinely guided process of canonization, the Bible can rightly be characterized as the result of God's rule (Canon). God gave His Word and preserved it from destruction and corruption so that our Scriptures are reliable.

Chapter 5

ILLUMINATION
AND
INTERPRETATION
OF
SCRIPTURE

The Holy Spirit is the author, preserver, and interpreter of the Scriptures. The Spirit has inspired the Scriptures and guided the church in collecting and placing the 66 books in our Bible. But more than this, the supreme authority for illuminating (shedding light upon) and interpreting Scripture belongs to the Holy Spirit. Convinced of this truth, Pentecostals rely on the Holy Spirit for understanding of the Scriptures. They see the Scriptures as the sword of the Spirit and believe that only through the Spirit can the heart of the biblical message be penetrated. By the work of the Holy Spirit in our hearts and minds, the truth spoken by the prophets and apostles can be personally understood and appropriated.

The Spirit's Illumination of Scripture

The inner illuminating witness of the Spirit causes the

Word of God to touch our hearts. The Scriptures teach that the gospel comes both in word and in the Holy Spirit (1 Thessalonians 1:5).

A. The Holy Spirit and the Written Word

The Spirit takes this Word, the gospel, and makes it a personal reality in our hearts. The Word of God is graphically described as "the sword of the Spirit" (Ephesians 6:17). The Holy Scripture is the Spirit's instrument, and the Scripture is effective only as the Holy Spirit wields it. God wills that we use "the sword of the Spirit," but not on our own authority or in our own power. We are to be completely open to the direction of the Holy Spirit as we wield His sword. Unless the Spirit wields this sword, it is wielded to no avail.

To put it another way, the Holy Spirit is vital to the working of the Word, and the Word is vital to the working of the Holy Spirit. Through His powerful inward ministry in our hearts, the Holy Spirit works with the written Word and illuminates the truth of the gospel. Divine truth may come to us in song, in testimony, in sermon, or through spiritual gifts; but all such means take us back to the written Word.

The bond of union between the Holy Spirit and the Word of God is strong. To try to isolate the Holy Spirit from sacred Scripture, or sacred Scripture from the Holy Spirit, is a mistake. The Spirit uses the Word to bring to us the knowledge of God's saving truth. We are led to faith, to Jesus Christ, and to eternal life only as the Holy Spirit works along with Holy Scripture.

The Word of God is not an independent power separated from the Holy Spirit. Isaiah 55:11 and Hebrews 4:12 speak of the power of the Word of God, but these are to be interpreted in light of the union of the Holy Spirit and the Word. The Holy Spirit illuminates the Word and makes it powerful so that it does not return to God empty. By the Spirit, God gives life, power, and light to His written Word and makes it powerfully persuasive to our souls. The Spirit's role is indispensable for illuminating and interpreting the divinely given writings. Only through the great revealer, the Holy Spirit, do we come to grips with the truth of Scripture.

B. The Spirit and the Preached Word

By no means does the witness of the Holy Spirit minimize the importance of our witness. He is the author of all witnessing and confronts us with the truth of God that we might bear witness to it. He made the apostles and prophets witnesses and through them created the written Word. Divine inspiration granted by the Spirit to the prophets and apostles was indispensable to their proclamation of divine truth. The same Spirit also now works both in the preacher and in the hearer.

The understanding of the divine message as it is preached flows from the illumination of the Spirit. The preaching of the Word is effective only when it is accompanied by the teaching of the Spirit. The secret revelation of the Spirit and His gracious work in our hearts enable our minds to understand the preached Word and enable us to submit our wills to its yoke.

The Spirit is the great teacher and revealer. He removes the veil from our hearts and enlightens the eyes of our understanding so that we can truly comprehend the truth of the written and preached Word. Only the divine light of the Spirit can drive away the darkness of sinful ignorance and reveal to us the deep things of God. This is precisely the teaching of Scripture. "But as it is written: *'Eye has not seen, nor ear heard, nor have entered into the heart of man the things which God has prepared for those who love*

Him'" (1 Corinthians 2:9). This truth is illustrated by the two disciples on the road to Emmaus (Luke 24:13-35). When our Lord appeared to them, they did not understand or believe in His saving death and resurrection. But as the Lord expounded the Scriptures to them, the Holy Spirit made their hearts burn within them, and their eyes were opened to the understanding that everything that happened to Jesus was in agreement with the prophetic Word and that He was the promised Redeemer. The inner work of the Spirit opens the eyes of the mind, moves the heart, and turns it toward God so that we may believe.

There is no conflict or discrepancy between the witness of the Holy Spirit and the Word of God. A Christian can misunderstand divine guidance and misinterpret Scripture, but the Spirit never misguides anyone. Only according to truth does He bear witness. The Holy Spirit neither constructs revelations contrary to the Word of God nor belittles the Scripture. Any doctrine or teaching that is not in harmony with the gospel is not of the Spirit of Truth.

The Holy Spirit and the Interpretation of Scripture

As Pentecostals study and interpret Scripture, they expect to hear a word from the Lord. For them, no method of Bible study is satisfactory unless it enables a person to receive a genuine word from God. Because of their understanding of the nature and function of Scripture, Pentecostals take unique approaches to the interpretation of the biblical text.

A. Pneumatic Interpretation

The Pentecostal approach to the interpretation of Scripture is pneumatic, that is, the interpreter relies on the illumination of the Spirit to come to a full understanding of the Scripture. *The basic principle of interpretation is that what has been written down by the inspiration of the Holy Spirit must be interpreted by the guidance of the same Spirit.* Through the experience of the Holy Spirit, modern readers span the time and cultural differences between them and the ancient author. Between the modern reader's experience and the apostolic experience, there is a common kinship. The common experience of the ancient author and modern reader lies in their shared faith in Christ and in their walk in the Spirit, whom the exalted Lord poured out at Pentecost (Acts 2:33). Faith provides the context in which Pentecostals interpret the Bible.

Pentecostals have a distinct view of knowledge. Knowledge is not viewed as merely an intellectual understanding of a set of truths, but as a knowing relationship with the One who established the truths by which we live. The teachings of Scripture remain unclear until the Holy Spirit illuminates human understanding to the mysteries of the gospel. Such a pneumatic view of knowledge finds its roots in Scripture (1 Corinthians 2:10). Believers come to know God through their walk in fellowship with the Spirit. Their faith is more than an intellectual acceptance of biblical doctrines; it is their response to living in relationship with the Holy Spirit. Consequently, believers come to know the Word of God as they live in relationship with its divine author, the Spirit of God.

B. Personal Experience

By the fresh outpouring of the Spirit on the 20th-century church, Pentecostals share in the experience of apostolic believers. The personal experience of Pentecost informs their interpretation of Scripture. *Pentecostal believers do not study the Bible in a detached manner.* Through the Spirit *they have entered into the expe-*

rience of the first-century Christians. They have received "their Pentecost" and have appropriated into their lives the experiences of Acts 2. But the place given to personal experience does not lead Pentecostals to disregard the historical context of Scripture. Pentecostals preserve the historical significance of the biblical text because it is precisely the significance of that history that the Holy Spirit re-creates for them. They see an undeniable connection between their experiences and that of apostolic believers. They also expect God's presence to be the same today as in Bible times. All the miraculous works of the Holy Spirit are understood to occur now as they did in the first-century church. Therefore, contemporary Pentecostals now live, through their own experience, the Pentecostal experience of the New Testament believers.

Two Dangers in Interpretation by Personal Experience

Pentecostals stress sensitivity to the Spirit's illumination and personal experience as aids to interpretation of the Bible. While such emphases are biblically sound, they are not without danger.

A. The Misguided May Confuse His Own Spirit (or Some Other Spirit) With the Holy Spirit

Because an interpreter claims divine guidance, his interpretation may be thought to be inerrant and on the level of Scripture. This assumption appears to render the interpretation itself inspired, infallible, and authoritative for faith and practice. However, it is dangerous to accept any interpretation without being sure it is in agreement with Scripture. Some people who have claimed to be led by the Spirit have, in fact, advocated heretical doctrines. What they thought was the leading of the Spirit was not the Spirit's help at all. Their approach was completely subjective. They failed to compare Scripture with Scripture and to listen to the Spirit as He has spoken to other interpreters of Scripture over the centuries.

Excesses are not necessarily the outcome of pneumatic interpretation. Pentecostals recognize that whenever interpretation of Scripture occurs, it is imperative that we "test the spirits" (1 John 4:1). *In fact, the spiritual dimension of interpretation does not give the interpreter free reign to interpret Scripture as he pleases. Pentecostals place the task of interpretation within the community of faith.* No one has the right to private interpretation without accountability. The proper exercise of pneumatic interpretation forces the interpreter to relate his spiritual illumination to the insight the Holy Spirit has afforded other believers of all ages and, particularly, the insight afforded the Pentecostal community. The true Pentecostal interpreter avoids spiritualizing and giving allegorical interpretations to Scripture. Instead, they respond to the Spirit's illumination so that His interpretation of God's Word is in accord with the life of the Spirit in the church.

B. The Misguided Interpreter May Make Personal Experience the Starting Point of Interpretation of Scripture

Pentecostal doctrines are not derived from personal experience but from the study of the Bible. Personal experience plays a rightful part in interpreting Scripture, but it is not the basis for Pentecostal interpretation and theology. It is true that God communicates revelation through personal experience as well as through Scripture. But *when personal experience is given the first place in the process of interpretation, it tends to usurp biblical authority and to displace the Scripture as the standard for the Christian life.* The inevitable result is that interpretation is directed toward justifying personal experience.

Responsible Pentecostal interpreters begin with the Scripture. Their conclusions are based on the interpretation of the Bible; but as is expected, personal experience may either confirm or deny those conclusions. Consequently, the historical narratives of the Old Testament may be used for the purpose of teaching New Testament Christians. Paul said the experiences of Israel "happened to them as examples, and they were written for our admonition" (1 Corinthians 10:11; cf. Galatians 4:21-31; 2 Timothy 3:16, 17). Aware that biblical history provides a basis for doctrine, Pentecostals appeal to the narrative of Acts not simply as history but also as doctrine. Throughout Acts, Luke's intent was to teach doctrine. In fact, Luke's account of the Jerusalem Council in Acts 15 provides Pentecostals with a model for interpretation of Scripture.

The Central Role of the Holy Spirit

At the Jerusalem Council, believers gathered around the Word of God in the power of the Spirit. Their purpose was to address a theological question about what was required of the Gentiles for salvation. Were the works of law, such as circumcision, needed, or was faith in Christ alone sufficient? At the meeting were representatives from the two local churches in Antioch and Jerusalem. That meeting was truly a Pentecostal meeting, in that the decision of the Council was corporate response to the Holy Spirit. As a result, James was able to declare, "For it seemed good to the Holy Spirit, and to us" (Acts 15:28). These words strongly indicate that early believers lived in the power of Pentecost. They thought and spoke under the guidance of the Holy Spirit. The activity of the Holy Spirit in the

Jerusalem Council, as well as in other examples of the Spirit's guidance in the New Testament, underscores the importance of the Holy Spirit to the interpretation of Scripture and to the whole life of the church. The sensitivity of the Council to the Holy Spirit enabled the believers to submit to His authority and to reach a common position.

Deliberations Guided by Scripture

In the Jerusalem Council, different speakers appealed to the Scriptures, experience, tradition, and reason. James asserted that Scripture fully agreed with Peter's argument that God had made provisions for the salvation of the Gentiles. In fact, all the prophets, particularly Amos, taught that God's eternal purpose was to include the Gentiles in His family (Acts 15:14-18; cf. Amos 9:11, 12). Paul and Barnabas told of their missionary experience in preaching the gospel. Their ministry had been attested by miracles and the conversion of large numbers of Gentiles (Acts 15:3, 4). Peter reminded the council of his personal call to preach to the Gentiles and related the experience of Cornelius and his friends when they were baptized in the Spirit (vv. 7-11). James appealed to a tradition rooted in Scripture, namely, regulations for strangers among Israelites (vv. 9-21; cf. Leviticus 17; 18). That tradition was the ground for his asking the Gentiles to observe the four prohibitions. Because the Gentiles had been purified by faith and the Spirit had been poured out on them, Peter reasoned that they should be accepted into the church (vv. 8-11). Likewise, James reasoned on the basis of Scripture and tradition that circumcision should not be required of Gentile believers.

The council's decision rested on Scripture, experience, tradition, and reason. Addressing issues from these perspectives, and under the guidance of the Spirit, provides a model for a

Pentecostal approach to Scripture and theological concerns. Out of the Pentecostal reality of the Spirit's being "poured out on all flesh" (Acts 2:17) emerges a distinctly Pentecostal approach to Scripture.

A Pentecostal Approach and the Use of Principles of Biblical Interpretation

The use of correct principles in the interpretation of Scripture is certainly valid for the Pentecostal. The accuracy of scriptural interpretation is enhanced by a detailed analysis of the biblical text. A careful study of a passage provides data for the Spirit to use to bring an accurate understanding of the truth. Features of such a study include the following principles of interpretation: *First, interpret the passage historically.* To understand a passage in its context the time, place, and intent of the author are important. *Second, interpret the passage grammatically.* The exact meaning of words, style, and construction are vital to determining the truth that is conveyed. *Third, interpret the immediate passage in light of the wider context.* When Scripture is compared with Scripture, the interpretation is likely to be sound and agree with the central doctrines of the Christian faith. *Fourth, consult the commentaries and expositions of learned interpreters who support the authority of Scripture and who are marked by spiritual depth and personal integrity.*

The Pentecostal approach to Scripture goes beyond the application of scriptural principles of interpretation and the recognition of truth. Scripture is not merely treated as an object we interpret but as the living Word which interprets us and through which flows the Spirit in ways that astound us and that we cannot dictate or program. *Pentecostal Bible study involves an interplay between knowledge of the truth and an overt response to the transforming call of God's Word.* The Spirit calls every believer to be a witness (Acts 1:8) and to participate in the community of faith. It is within the fellowship of believers that Pentecostal faith is nurtured and sustained. It is also within the fellowship of believers that there are bonds of mutual love and accountability, and there is a context for the practice of the Pentecostal approach to Scripture that will "not put out the Spirit's fire" (1 Thessalonians 5:19, *NIV*).

Part Two:

DOCTRINE

OF

GOD

Chapter 6

IDENTITY
OF THE
TRUE GOD

Who is God? What does it mean to say, "God"? These questions have been answered in various ways. As a result the term God (or god) can have many meanings. Anything that is considered by us to be the most important in our life can be called our "god." However, the worship of anything or any person other than the God of the Bible is idolatry—the worship of an idol.

Needless to say there are many religious and philosophical views of God. The term *God* may be ascribed to an ideal or an impersonal power. But when Pentecostals speak of God, they mean the God of the Bible, not the God of human speculation but the living God of Abraham, Isaac, and Jacob—the God and Father of our Lord Jesus Christ. *The God of the Bible has revealed Himself in Jesus Christ and has revealed Himself to our* hearts by the Holy Spirit. Through the Spirit we experience His presence and worship Him. In a sense God is beyond our understanding, but God has revealed Himself in ways that we can understand. Even so, it would be a mistake to think of God as an object that we grasp as other objects in the world.

In our discussion of the doctrine of Scripture and revelation we dealt with the issue of how God is truly known. Now, we move on to the question of who God is and what He is like. At the heart of the Christian faith stands the doctrine of God. So to understand, as far as possible, the character and nature of God is basic to the entire fabric of Christian theology. For the understanding of God we turn to the Scriptures.

God Is Real

Nowhere does the Bible attempt to prove there is a God. Rather, Scripture assumes the existence of God from its opening words: "In the beginning God. . . ." Wherever God is named in Scripture, it is understood that He exists. The psalmist felt that God's existence was something so clearly seen that no one but a fool says in his heart, "There is no God" (Psalm 14:1).

At the burning bush God offered no explanation to Moses for His existence. Moses inquired of God what he should say when the Israelites asked who had sent him. God's only reply was, "I AM WHO I AM" (Exodus 3:14). In other places in the Old Testament, God reveals Himself as "I AM." So we read, "I am the LORD your God, who brought you out of the land of Egypt (20:2); and "I, even I, am He who comforts you" (Isaiah 51:12; cf. Deuteronomy 32:39). The divine name "I AM" represents the majesty and the self-sufficiency of the one true God who is constant in His faithfulness to His people. But He requires no explanation for His existence. There is no source from which He has come.

According to the whole Bible, God exists, lives, acts, and makes Himself known. Philosophers and theologians have attempted to prove God. But the Bible speaks of One who needs no proof and who proves Himself by His revelation and mighty works. Israel could not doubt the reality of God after their deliverance from Egyptian bondage. The divine calls of Isaiah and Jeremiah to ministry were decisive encounters with the living God (Isaiah 6:1-8; Jeremiah 1:4-10). Likewise, Paul had a profound experience of God on the road to Damascus (Acts 26:12-18). To each of these men God revealed Himself in a different way, but they had an unforgettable experience of the real God, who made them His chosen vessels.

God is described in Holy Scripture as unsearchable, that is, He has not been found by our searching for Him. But when we seek Him, we find that He has disclosed Himself to us. Through the created universe God has revealed something about Himself, namely, "His eternal power and Godhead" (Romans 1:20). The Scriptures, which are God's own word of testimony, are a better source for our knowledge of Him. The aim of God's disclosure of Himself is not primarily to satisfy human curiosity or to prove His existence. It is to heal the broken relationship between us and our Creator. So the reality of God's existence should affect profoundly our whole view of the world and the way we live in it.

Even a deeper truth is that the living God has entered into the lives of His creatures. *God has appeared among us in His Son, Jesus Christ. In Christ the depth of God's being and saving purpose are manifested.* There is no deeper knowledge of God than what He revealed in the Cross of His beloved Son. At Golgotha the Father laid His heart open and brought into full view His love. *Emmanuel,* "God with us," affords us a personal knowledge of God. This profound insight is revealed in Jesus' words as He prayed, "And this is eternal life, that they may know You, the only true God, and Jesus Christ whom You have sent" (John 17:3).

God Is Spirit

Scripture makes no attempt to define God. The closest it comes to a description of God is where Jesus said, "God is Spirit" (John 4:24). Doubtlessly these words mean that God's essential nature is spirit. A spirit is real but does not have a body such as we have. We must not think of God as physically limited in any way to places or things. God does not have a physical body like ours. He is spiritual, invisible, and is not limited by time or space (John 1:18; 1 Timothy 1:17; 6:16).

When we say God is [a] Spirit, we mean that His manner of existence is infinitely different from our existence as physical creatures. The term *Spirit*, as applied to God, may have a broad meaning but can be used also in a more restricted sense for that person of the Trinity, the Holy Spirit. Broadly applied, the word *Spirit* refers to God, indicating His spirituality and His existence on an infinitely higher level than ours. He is free of all limitations associated with corporal existence. Not limited to time or space, He is present everywhere at once and is eternal Spirit. What is spiritual is ultimately real and lasting. From everlasting to everlasting God is Spirit.

God Is Living

The Bible characterizes God as the living God (Joshua 3:10; Hosea 1:10; 1 Timothy 3:15; Hebrews 9:14; 10:31). This understanding of God distinguished Him from Baal and other pagan gods. The Hebrews encountered Him in the events of their history as the living God. A common way to introduce a vow was with the words "As the LORD lives" (Judges 8:19). God swears by His own life (Numbers 14:21). *God* and *life* belong together, for Scripture admits of no God of the dead but only the God of the living (Mark 12:27). *God is the "fountain of life" (Psalm 36:9). He has life in Himself and His life did not come from another. He gives life, creates the creature, and renews the face of the earth. All life stems from Him and remains dependent on Him.* Jesus spoke of God the Father as having life in Himself (John 5:26). God is the One "who gives life to all things" (1 Timothy 6:13). No creature has life in itself; all life is a gift of God.

God formed man from the dust of the ground and breathed divine breath into his lifeless body so that he became a living person. Though Adam shared biological life with the animal creation, he was uniquely created in the image of God, with spiritual life, and therefore had the capability of a personal relationship with the living God. Jesus recognized that all human beings have the potential for spiritual life; but He also recognized that sinners live as though they are not created in the image of God. Such a bare, physical existence falls far short of what God intends for mankind.

Physical life has been transmitted from Adam to us. But the last Adam, the resurrected Jesus Christ, is "a life-giving spirit. . . . the Lord from heaven" (1 Corinthians 15:45, 47). What Christ bestows is the gift of eternal life. It is an abundant, overflowing experience of the living God, who alone has immortality. God's immortality and our mortality were united in Jesus Christ. At His first coming, Christ died for us and arose from the dead. Thereby He "abolished death and brought life and immortality to light through the gospel" (2 Timothy 1:10).

God Is Personal

God is invisible, but He is not merely a vapor or an impersonal force. He is a personal Spirit. The personal aspect of God's being is central to biblical revelation. *Only a personal God has powers of thought, affection, and will. Only a personal God can plan, make, and carry out decisions; love and disapprove. Throughout the Bible God is described as One who thinks, feels, and directs His own activities.* For example, the psalmist exclaimed, "He does whatever He pleases" (Psalm 115:3). His activity is consistently described as purposeful, thereby demonstrating His intelligence and therefore His personality. So we read that God chose Israel to be a special people (Deuteronomy 7:6-8). He feels joy, sorrow, and anger as He looks on His people. The psalmist said, "God is angry with the wicked every day" (Psalm 7:11). His loving-kindness and tender mercies set forth in the Psalms are too numerous to mention. Furthermore, from the first book of the Bible to the last, God talks and communes with His children. The account of Adam's creation bears witness to God's personality. God created him in His own image. A God without personality would have been incapable of creating persons.

Of all the personal names that appear in Scripture for God, none of them reminds us more of His deeply personal character than the name *Father.* The personal designation of God as Father is rare in the Old Testament. The prophet Isaiah cried out, "O LORD, You are our Father" (64:8). The fatherhood of God is frequently implied in such statements as "Thus says the LORD: 'Israel is My son, My firstborn'" (Exodus 4:22) and "When Israel was a child, I loved him, and out of Egypt I called My son" (Hosea 11:1). God entered into a very personal relationship with the nation of Israel, and they were viewed as His children. Many of the psalms emphasize an intimate fellowship between God and the devout among His people.

As the divine Son of God, Jesus referred to God often with

the intensely personal designation *Father*. His first recorded words revealed that He must be about His Father's business (Luke 2:49), and His last words on the earth were concerned with the promise of His Father that believers would be endowed with power from on high (24:49). He taught His disciples to pray, "Our Father in heaven" (Matthew 6:9). In the parable of the prodigal son, Jesus showed the heavenly Father's care and love. It is not uncommon in the New Testament for God to be spoken of as the Father of all people in the sense of being Creator and Sustainer of all. All people are objects of His gracious care.

Jesus also taught that God was uniquely His Father (John 5:18), and rightly so since He was identified as the "only begotten of the Father" (1:14). *The Son manifested the heart of the Father, laying open the redemptive desire of God to the eyes of men and women.* The early Christians came to speak of God as the "Father of our Lord Jesus Christ" (2 Corinthians 11:31; Colossians 1:3). That, of course, is true, but the full significance of God as Father is seen in the redemptive work of Christ. All who believe in Jesus Christ are "born again" and become God's adopted children. They enter a personal relationship with God that goes immeasurably beyond our relation with Him as Creator and Sustainer of life. As children of God, we are heirs of God and joint heirs with the Son. *God has shown Himself to be uniquely personal by the life and redemptive work of Jesus Christ.* And, too, through the inner witness of the Spirit arises an intimate, personal knowledge of God as Father. In making us His children, "God has sent forth the Spirit of His Son into . . . [our] hearts, crying out, 'Abba, Father!'" (Galatians 4:6).

It is very important that we think of God as personal and as our heavenly Father. Otherwise we may treat God as an impersonal object rather than as a personal subject. *The warm faith of*

Pentecostals centers in the personal dimensions of God. We do not see ourselves as standing over God to study Him but as in relationship with Him to enjoy and obey Him. God is alive, personally concerned about His people. He hears and answers prayer. He is involved in our personal lives and stories. He is, therefore, capable of entering into our sorrows and joys. The God of Calvary has opened His heart and mind to us in the Scriptures; and the heavenly Father, in the person of His Son, has entered into human pain and sorrow. He empathizes with human suffering, and we can walk and talk with Him. This is the kind of God He is.

God Is One

From beginning to end the Bible teaches that there is only one God. "Hear, O Israel: The LORD our God, the LORD is one!" (Deuteronomy 6:4). "I am the LORD your God. . . . You shall have no other gods before Me" (Exodus 20:2, 3). "Before Me there was no God formed, nor shall there be after Me" (Isaiah 43:10). Again and again the prophets warned the people of Israel against the worship of other gods. A basic theme of their message was that God is and God is one. He is the First and the Last; besides Him there is no God (Isaiah 44:6).

The New Testament affirms the same thing. When Jesus was asked what was the first and greatest commandment, He repeated the ancient creed of Israel: "Hear, O Israel, the LORD our God, the LORD is one. And you shall love the LORD your God with all your heart, with all your soul, with all your mind, and with all your strength" (Mark 12:29, 30). He responded to the rich young ruler who addressed Him as "Good Teacher" with the sharp statement "No one is good but One, that is, God" (Mark 10:18). And other New Testament passages say, "There is no other God but one" (1 Corinthians 8:4), and there is "one God and Father of all" (Ephesians 4:6). The confession of the one God permeates the whole of Scripture.

That God is one summarizes the faith of Christians throughout the ages. God is not one among many gods but the one God. "One" refers to His unity. He is a single and undivided Being. God cannot be divided. The true God is a unified Being. Jesus Christ himself reminds us of the essential unity of God. According to John 17:22 He prayed to His Father "that they [believers] may be one just as We are one." The Lord Jesus was on the earth praying to the Father in heaven. Yet His words "We are one" affirmed the perfect unity between Him and the Father. So there is only one God.

Over against the gods and lords of this world, the God of Scripture stands as the one true God, the only Creator and Lord of the universe. Christians have been set free from the superstition and slavery of believing in many gods so that they may love and serve the one true God.

Under no circumstances can we allow other gods to stand alongside God and claim the devotion that He alone deserves. Before Him are to be no other gods. That includes not only primitive gods of stone, wood, and gold but also such modern gods as self, power, prestige, position, pleasure, wealth, and success. The gods of this age are to be renounced, and we are to serve the one God whose claim on our lives is total and exclusive. Faith in Christ calls for us to trust and obey the one true God who eternally exists in three persons—Father, Son, and Holy Spirit.

Chapter 7

NAMES
OF
GOD

What is God like? A study of God's names can help us to answer this question. Often in the Bible a name indicated a person's character and function. The character and ministry of the coming Messiah was depicted by the names *Immanuel, Wonderful, Counselor, Mighty God, Everlasting Father, Prince of Peace* (Isaiah 7:14; 9:6). On the basis of his covenant relationship with God, *Abram* ("exalted father") was changed to *Abraham* ("father of a multitude"). *Jacob* ("supplanter") became *Israel* ("he perseveres with God"), after his encounter with God at the river Jabbok (Genesis 32:28). The change of Simon's name to *Peter* pointed to his new character as "the rock man" (John 1:42).

A variety of names for God appear in Scripture. The names that identify God were not simply given to Him by His people; they were divinely revealed. His names embody facets of His own disclosure of Himself. Each of the names makes manifest certain aspects of God's character and power. But no one of the divine names alone is adequate to express God's greatness. If the heavens cannot contain Him, how can one name describe Him?

At places in Scripture, God's name is protected with the commandment "You shall not take the name of the LORD your God in vain" (Exodus 20:7). This forbids misuse of any of the names ascribed to God. God is to be held in respect and reverence, and so are His names, since they reveal His character.

Pentecostals believe the names of God in the Old Testament find their complement and fulfillment in the person and work of Jesus Christ, who is the brightness of God's glory and "the express image of His person" (Hebrews 1:3), and in whom "dwells all the fullness of the Godhead bodily" (Colossians 2:9). Let us look at a number of the names by which God has revealed Himself.

Jehovah (Yahweh)

The term is, of course, a very common name of God in the Old Testament. *Jehovah* (or *LORD*) appears 6,823 times in the Old Testament and is an intensely personal name. Through this name, God disclosed Himself to Israel, His people, and made it clear to them the possibility of knowing Him as a person.

A. Meaning of the Name

As transliterated from the Hebrew Old Testament, the four letters *YHWH*, when supplied with vowels, is *Yahweh (Jehovah)*. For the Jews, Jehovah was the most sacred of the names of God. It literally means "He Who Is," for God is the essence of all being. So when we read the name *Jehovah* in the Bible, we should think of being, existence, and life. God exists as no other being exists. He is eternally self-existent and is the source of all life. When God confronted Moses at the burning bush, He defined the name *Jehovah*. This revealed name was explained by the well-known phrase "I AM WHO I AM" (Exodus 3:14). The "I AM" who spoke to Moses at the burning bush was no new God but the living God who had been worshiped by Abraham, Isaac, and Jacob and who said, "This [Jehovah] is my name forever" (v. 15). He is the One who promised to be with His people and to deliver them from bondage (vv. 16-22).

B. Significance of the Name

The name *Jehovah* was tied closely to Israel's spiritual experience and was a means of special revelation. At the Exodus, Jehovah revealed Himself by His mighty acts and called His people out of Egypt. These mighty acts were "redemptive acts." The Hebrews entered into a covenant relationship with Jehovah, who intervened in their lives at a time of greatest need and redeemed them from Egyptian bondage. Therefore the Ten Commandments are prefaced with this reminder: "I am the LORD [Jehovah] your God, who brought you out of the land of Egypt, out of the house of bondage" (Exodus 20:2).

Again we see His saving work under the name *Jehovah* in Exodus 33:19. God said to Moses, "I will make all My goodness pass before you, and I will proclaim the name of the LORD [Jehovah] before you. I will be gracious to whom I will be gracious, and I will have compassion on whom I will have compassion." Jehovah made Himself known to a chosen nation of the human race, the Jews. To them He began to demonstrate His desire to show mercy not only to the Jews but also to the entire human family.

For the Jews the divine name *Jehovah* was held in such awe that they feared mispronouncing it. So when they came to this name in the Old Testament, they would say instead *Adonai* (*Lord*) in its place. Though there was reluctance on the part of the Jews to speak His holy name, Jehovah was understood to be distinctively personal and the One who made a covenant relationship with His people. He, the entirely self-existent being, was at the same time concerned with His children and desired to have fellowship with them.

The name *Jehovah* appears only in the Old Testament. But we have strong reason to believe that Jesus picked up the significance of the name *Jehovah*, especially when He used the emphatic form "I am" (Greek: *Ego eimi*) in the Gospels. He said, "Before Abraham was, I AM" (John 8:58). So He identified Himself with Jehovah who declared in Exodus 3:14, "I AM WHO I AM." When Jesus declared Himself to be the "I AM," the Jews knew He claimed to be God. He declared Himself the "I AM" who forgives sin: "If you do not believe that I am He, you will die in your sins" (John 8:24). Only God himself can forgive sin. In Jesus Christ was fulfilled the ultimate significance of the name *Jehovah*. He manifested Himself as the only means of redemption from sin (Acts 4:12).

Elohim—A Name for God

The first words of the Bible are "In the beginning God created . . ." (Genesis 1:1). Here the Hebrew word for God is *Elohim*. However, in the King James Version, *Elohim* is frequently translated *Lord*. The name *Elohim* is plural, signifying plurality of majesty or greatness. The plural was used because the singular form (*El*) was not adequate to express the fullness of God. The plural suggests the fullness of the Godhead.

A. Meaning of the Name

The way *Elohim* is applied to God depicts Him as One who has great power and strength. He is the all-powerful God, for we are told that "the LORD your God [Elohim] is God of gods and Lord of lords, the great God, mighty and awesome" (Deuteronomy 10:17). Elohim, by His mighty power, created the universe. Elohim speaks and it is done. He brings into existence what was not, calls forth light out of darkness, and creates life in His image. Elohim made great and mighty promises to Abraham and Jacob (Genesis 17:1; 35:11). Elohim made a covenant with Abraham; and because He could swear by no one greater, He swore by Himself.

Before his death, Joseph assured the people of Israel that Elohim would deliver them from Egypt and bring them into the land promised to Abraham, Isaac, and Jacob (Genesis 50:24). So *Elohim*, as a name of God, establishes the fact of His absolute strength and might. He has demonstrated His absolute power by His wonderful acts—creating and ruling the universe and making a covenant and keeping it with His servants who walk before Him with all their heart (1 Kings 8:23).

B.   Significance of the Name

As already observed, the identification of God as Elohim suggests power and authority. This truth is revealed not only in all of creation, animate and inanimate, as the work of Elohim, but also in the fact that He is the ruler of the whole creation. Besides that, the supreme power of Elohim is seen in His initiation and perpetuation of a covenant to redeem creation. But the significance of Elohim even goes beyond the idea of an all-sufficient God for His creation.

It is no mere coincidence that the plural form *Elohim* is a name for the "one God." *Elohim* suggests diversity and richness in God's own existence. For although *Elohim* is plural, it is, nevertheless, often accompanied by verbs, adjectives, and pronouns in the singular, showing that God, diverse and rich in His very essence, is one. A good example is Deuteronomy 32:39:

"Now see that I, even I, am He, and there is no God [*Elohim*] besides Me."

At the same time, the name *Elohim* prepared the way for the later revelation of the Trinity. Since the plural indicates the fullness of God, *Elohim* also stood for the Godhead. It was the triune Godhead who asked the prophet Isaiah, "Who will go for Us?" (6:8). So the New Testament disclosure of three persons (Father, Son, and Holy Spirit) within the one God did not appear as altogether new in the first century. The name Elohim intimated a rich diversity in God and anticipated the revelation of the Holy Trinity. The second person of the Godhead, Jesus Christ, said, "All authority has been given to Me in heaven and on earth" (Matthew 28:18). The omnipotence of Elohim became visible in the miracles and saving power of Jesus Christ and will ultimately be realized in His rule over all powers and principalities until all enemies are under His feet (Ephesians 1:20-22; Hebrews 1:13).

Adonai—Another Word for Lord

So far the two names of God we have examined relate to the person of God. *Jehovah* signifies His self-existence and *Elohim* His omnipotence. These names imply our responsibility to obey God. But now we consider a third name, *Adonai*, by which God makes a definite claim upon our obedience.

A. Meaning of the Name

Essentially, *Adonai* means "Lord." The singular form, *adon*, is used only of men and is usually translated "master," "sir," or "lord." Throughout Genesis 24, Eliezer the servant of Abraham speaks of "my master [*adon*] Abraham." The plural form, *Adonai*, is reserved as a name for God and points to the idea of the Trinity as is also found in the name *Elohim*. A passage in which Adonai appears and strikingly suggests that God is more than one person is Psalm 110:1, where David said, "The LORD [Jehovah] said to my Lord [Adon], 'Sit at My right hand, till I make Your enemies Your footstool.'" Hence, there is the suggestion of a second person alongside Jehovah. It is significant that the Lord Jesus clearly applied the striking words of Psalm 110:1 to Himself (Matthew 22:41-45; Mark 12:35-37; Luke 20:41-44; cf. Acts 2:34, 35). So speaking of one person, David used the singular form *Adon*—"Jehovah said to Adon," that is, to Christ, the second person of the triune God. Without doubt Adonai signifies divine lordship or mastership. But the full meaning of this name cannot be grasped apart from seeing it as pointing in the direction that God is always three-in-one and one-in-three. The Great Three-in-One are Father, Son, and Holy Spirit.

B. Significance of the Name

As Lord, Adonai has a right to the obedience and service of His people. This relationship can be seen when God appeared to Abraham in a vision. Abraham addressed Him as Adonai-Jehovah ("Lord GOD," Genesis 15:2). That meant that Jehovah was his Master and that he was Jehovah's slave. The slave in those days had privileges and rights. Among the Jews a hired servant could not eat of the Passover because he was considered a stranger. But the slave had the privilege of celebrating the Passover, for he was a member of his master's family (Exodus 12:43-45). He also had the right to his master's protection and help, and it was not uncommon for the master-slave relationship to be one of affection (Deuteronomy 15:12-17; Psalm 123:2).

A human master could show love and be faithful to provide for the welfare of those who served him. This was also true with Adonai. The commission of Moses to deliver Israel from Egyptian bondage is an excellent example of divine provision. On that occasion Moses acknowledged God's right to his life and service when he addressed Him as Adonai. He pleaded, "O my

Lord [*Adonai*], I am not eloquent . . . I am slow of speech" (Exodus 4:10). The Lord gave Moses assurance that He would be his sufficiency. He never asked His servants to do a task without equipping them for it.

As in the Old Testament, so in the New, as Lord, God is One who bestows spiritual gifts and equips His people for service. On the Day of Pentecost, Peter declared that God exalted the crucified Jesus as Lord. He also declared that the Lord Jesus had equipped the disciples with the power of the Holy Spirit so they could bear witness of the gospel (Acts 1:8; 2:33-36). From that time the ascended, triumphant Christ gave gifts to His servants, making some apostles, others prophets, evangelists, pastors, teachers—all for "the equipping of the saints for the work of ministry, for the edifying of the body of Christ" (Ephesians 4:12). Having these gifts and others from our Lord, Paul exhorts us to be faithful servants and to exercise them with diligence (Romans 12:6-8).

The letters of the apostle Paul abound with references to the lordship of Jesus Christ. He saw all believers, including himself, as servants of Christ. He seems to have been delighted to emphasize the lordship of Christ by calling himself a bondservant of Christ. For him "servant of Christ" was a title of honor. As a servant of Christ, he bore in his own body the marks of the Lord Jesus (Galatians 6:17) and rendered total loyalty and unlimited service to his Lord. He genuinely felt that honor had been shown him by having the opportunity to serve his Adonai—his Master. Said he, "I thank Christ Jesus our Lord who has enabled me, because He counted me faithful, putting me into the ministry" (1 Timothy 1:12).

El Shaddai

As *El Shaddai*, God revealed Himself, especially during the patriarchal period. This name has a warm and personal connotation, indicating that God wants to help and bless His people.

A. Meaning of the Name

El Shaddai means "God Almighty." Power and might are associated with this name as they are with the name Elohim. Whereas Elohim refers to God as mighty Creator and Sustainer of the universe, El Shaddai views God as actively involved in the affairs of His people, shaping the forces of nature to accomplish His purpose. Obviously, the name El Shaddai consists of two words: (1) El is translated "God," signifying might, power, omnipotence; (2) Shaddai means "strong, powerful, almighty, all-sufficient." God's disclosure of Himself as God Almighty emphasizes that He is all-sufficient. That is, He is able to carry His plans to fulfillment and abundantly bless His people. He is able to do infinitely more than we ask or think.

B. Significance of the Name

Looking at the circumstances under which the name El Shaddai was first disclosed, we get a good idea of its significance. El Shaddai's activity among His people points to two truths.

First, El Shaddai is in control of the processes of nature and can set aside the ordinary course of nature. Abraham and Sarah were a good example of this. God promised to make Abraham a great nation (Genesis 12:2). But years passed and Sarah had no children. At the age of 99, it seemed impossible for Abraham to have a son, but God disclosed Himself as El Shaddai and confirmed the promise (17:1, 2). Though Abraham and Sarah were beyond the normal time of life for childbearing, the deadness of their bodies was overcome and Isaac was born. God Almighty governs all things. He can constrain natural processes and go beyond the ordinary in nature so that purposes of His grace are served. What He promises, He can give.

Second, El Shaddai is the God of inexhaustible blessings. He changed the name of *Abram* ("exalted father") to *Abraham*, which means "father of a multitude," and made a staggering promise to him: "I will make you exceedingly fruitful; and I will make nations of you, and kings shall come from you" (Genesis 17:6). At a later time Isaac blessed Jacob and said, "May God Almighty [*El Shaddai*] bless you, and make you fruitful and multiply you, that you may be an assembly of peoples" (28:3). God himself said to Jacob, "I am God Almighty [*El Shaddai*]. Be fruitful and multiply; a nation and a company of nations shall proceed from you, and kings shall come from your body" (35:11). On his deathbed Jacob repeated the blessings promised in the name of El Shaddai (48:3, 4), and in that name he pronounced on Joseph a shower of blessings of every kind (49:25).

Other examples could be cited, but we see that the name *God Almighty* reminds us of His inexhaustible blessings. The fullness and richness of His bounty are best seen in the outpouring of His love in Jesus Christ. So El Shaddai expresses that profound truth that the All-Sufficient One has a very personal interest in us and has manifested His mighty power to save and bless us by sending His Son into the world.

Jehovah-Rophe

God reveals Himself as the One who meets every need as it arises in the experience of His people. He saves, strengthens, sustains, sanctifies, and even heals them. This name of God, *Jehovah-Rophe*, became known in Israel's earliest experiences in the wilderness (Exodus 15:22-26). From the Red Sea they traveled for three days but found no water they could drink. Then at

Marah, God showed the Israelites a tree that would make the brackish, bitter waters suitable for drinking. When that tree of God was cast into the bitter waters, the waters were healed and sweetened. So God brought Israel into circumstances that tested their faith and obedience. And He said that if they would diligently obey Him, He would spare them of the diseases that came upon the Egyptians. Then He added, "For I am the LORD who heals you," that is, *Jehovah Rophe.*

A. Meaning of the Name

The word *rophe* appears numbers of times in the Old Testament and always means "to repair, to restore, and to heal." At times it refers to healing of physical diseases or disorders. But it is also used in a spiritual sense to speak of forgiveness of sin and restoration to divine favor. So out of the wilderness experience of Israel, as described in Exodus 15:22-26, came this comforting name of God, *Jehovah-Rophe*—"Jehovah heals." In Moses' time Jehovah promised His people He would be their healer on the condition of their obedience. However, this promise was not only for Israel but also for the redeemed of all ages. The things that happened to Israel, Paul said, were examples for us and "were written for our admonition, on whom the ends of the ages have come" (1 Corinthians 10:11).

B. Significance of the Name

Sickness, whether physical or spiritual, shows no partiality. Physical disorders and disease are rampant in the world. People are sick and in constant need of healing for their bodies. And the need of healing is even greater in the moral and spiritual realm. The ravages of sin and moral corruption have taken their toll on humanity. Pentecostals are keenly aware of the prevalence of physical and spiritual sickness on the earth. At the same time, they believe that prayer for those who are physically sick, as well as spiritually sick, is a vital part of the ministry of the church. For them the physician for ills of the flesh and spirit is Jehovah-Rophe. And this is the God who wrought mighty healings through Jesus Christ, His Son. God is Jehovah-Rophe.

First, He heals from sin by redemption from its awful consequences. The prophet Jeremiah identified the fundamental moral and spiritual sickness when he said that the human heart is "desperately wicked" (17:9). Sin has marred and corrupted humanity. It has alienated the human heart from God. The healer of the devastating disease of sin is Jehovah-Rophe. The psalmist acknowledged Him as the Healer: "Bless the LORD, O my soul . . . who forgives all your iniquities, who heals all your diseases" (103:2, 3).

In Scripture, many times sicknesses and wounds are figurative expressions of spiritual and moral ills. Such ills were what Jeremiah had in mind when he said, "'For I will restore health to you and heal your wounds,' says the LORD" (30:17). He also said, "Return, you backsliding children, and I will heal your backslidings" (3:22). Similarly, Isaiah wrote about the day in which "the LORD binds up the bruise of His people and heals the stroke of their wound" (30:26). He predicted the coming of Christ, on whom would rest the Spirit of the Lord, for Him "to heal the brokenhearted, to proclaim liberty to the captives" (61:1).

Jehovah desires to provide healing from every evil and salvation from every sin. Healing for all the hurts and wounds brought about by sin is in the hands of Jehovah. Accepting His grace of forgiveness makes us whole and delivers us from diseases of the heart and spirit. So often people go on rejecting Jehovah's healing power. That was what Jesus had in mind when He said, "You are not willing to come to Me that you may have life" (John 5:40).

Second, God has healed and still does heal many who are physically sick. The Old Testament tells of a number of occasions when the power of God was manifested to heal physical ailments. A notable example was that of Hezekiah, who was not only healed of a deadly illness but also granted an additional 15 years of life (2 Kings 20:1-7). When Miriam became leprous, Moses cried out, "Please heal her, O God, I pray!" (Numbers 12:13). God removed plagues and pestilences and healed not only Miriam but also Naaman, the Syrian general, of the dreaded disease of leprosy (2 Kings 5:1-14).

Jesus Christ performed the same kind of miraculous healings in His ministry. He not only healed the souls of people by forgiving their sins, He also healed fevers, cleansed lepers, and cast out demons. He went about "preaching the gospel of the kingdom, and healing all kinds of sickness and all kinds of disease among the people" (Matthew 4:23). His miracles of healing constantly amazed the people and bore witness of His identity and mission. Jesus said, "The works which the Father has given Me to finish . . . bear witness of Me, that the Father has sent Me" (John 5:36). Jesus returned in the power of the Spirit from the Temptation and set the pattern for His entire ministry by citing Isaiah 61:1, 2: "The Spirit of the LORD is upon Me, because He has anointed Me to preach the gospel to the poor. He has sent Me to heal the brokenhearted, to preach deliverance to the captives and recovery of sight to the blind, to set at liberty those who are oppressed, to preach the acceptable year of the LORD" (Luke 4:18, 19).

Jesus Christ is the Great Healer in both a spiritual and physical sense. Jehovah Rophe has demonstrated through His Son Jesus Christ that He can heal every disease. What Jehovah was to Israel at Marah, the Lord Jesus is now for God's people—the Great Physician.

Chapter 8

ATTRIBUTES
OF
GOD

The divine attributes (characteristics of God) point to the infinitely rich diversity in the one true God. From the Bible we learn what the living God is like. But the Scriptures never attempt to give a complete list of His attributes. God's activities and characteristics described in Scripture and reflected in creation do provide an understanding of His character. It is reassuring to know that the God of Scripture is present in our world and that He is the same God whom we have experienced in our individual lives through faith in Christ.

For Pentecostals, the Scriptures and the Holy Spirit's enlightenment of our minds are most important to grasping the various aspects of God's nature. To be sure, the Holy Spirit is the guide to our understanding, but only as we are immersed in the Word of God does the Spirit bring an understanding of the deep things of God. It is impossible to comprehend fully the living

God and His attributes, but all the attributes belong equally to the Father, Son, and Holy Spirit. The attributes of God have been classified in different ways, but it will be convenient to deal with them under two major headings: Divine Attributes Traceable in Humankind and Attributes Not Discernible in Humankind.

Divine Attributes Traceable in Humankind

God possesses certain characteristics or attributes that are reflected in His human creatures. These that are reflected in us are due to our being created in the image of God. Such attributes of God can be classified in three ways.

A. Intellectual Attributes
1. Knowledge

God is all-knowing. He has perfect knowledge of all that was or is or can be. He has no need to learn. We do not know tomorrow until tomorrow, but He knows it today. His knowledge encompasses the past, present, and future. Scripture teaches that God has never been taught by anyone. "Who has known the mind of the LORD? Or who has become His counselor?" (Romans 11:34; cf. Isaiah 40:13, 14). God has never sat at the feet of a teacher whether the teacher be highest cherub or archangel.

Basically the omniscience of God means two things: (1) At once God knows all things. No one could reveal anything about us to Him that He does not already know. The sons and daughters of Adam cannot hide their sins from Him (Hebrews 4:13). He knows the smallest details, even the number of hairs on our head (Luke 12:7). (2) God knows all things in and outside of Himself. His knowing is absolute. His knowledge is an eternal knowledge. Nothing has been added to God's knowledge and nothing can be.

Man's knowledge, limited as it is, is a dim reflection of God's infinite knowledge.

2. Wisdom

Knowledge is related to wisdom, but there is a difference. Wisdom is the application of knowledge. God uses the best means to accomplish the highest ends. He accomplishes His purpose by the use of the most worthy means. His wisdom is boundless, but ours is very small. For this reason both the apostle Paul and Jude spoke of "God who alone is wise" (1 Timothy 1:17; Jude 25). The wisdom of angels or people is only a reflection of God's wisdom. His works always achieve the highest and best. Nothing that He does can be improved. God sees all things in their proper perspective and is therefore able to effect flawless ends. He weighs all ends, knows all needs, comprehends all possibilities and understands all means.

By His wisdom God accomplishes His gracious and good purpose. The psalmist was amazed at God's wisdom in creation. "O LORD, how manifold are Your works! In wisdom You have made them all" (Psalm 104:24). It comes as no surprise that Paul saw the wisdom of God in the plan of salvation. He wrote, "Christ . . . the wisdom of God" (1 Corinthians 1:24). Jesus Christ, the perfect Savior, was chosen to achieve the perfect end—salvation for mankind. So wisdom is God's perfect adequacy for the administration of all affairs.

B. Moral Attributes

1. Goodness

God's goodness disposes Him to deal kindly and bountifully with His creatures. Like God's other attributes, His goodness is infinite, eternal, and unchangeable. God is just as good now as He has ever been and ever will be. He makes the sun to shine on both the good and the evil and sends rain on the just and the unjust (Matthew 5:45). The cause of God's goodness is God himself. His goodness is the ground for blessing the believer. Faith and obedience are evidence that the believer is convinced that God is good. The psalmist understood that God is good, for he said, "The LORD is good to all" (Psalm 145:9).

2. Love

The love of God is one of the great realities of the Christian faith. The apostle John declared, "God is love." But to say that God is love does not mean love is God. If God and love were identical, the worship of love would be the worship of God. The worship of love, however, would be idolatry. We worship God, not His attributes. Love does not account for the total being of God, but it is one attribute of God. Jesus Christ answers forever any question about God's love. "In this is love, not that we loved God, but that He loved us and sent His Son to be the propitiation [all-sufficient sacrifice] for our sins" (1 John 4:10). "But God demonstrates His own love toward us, in that while we were still sinners, Christ died for us" (Romans 5:8). So to know the love of God is to know Christ in His saving action toward us.

God's great love became visible in the sending of His Son and His Son's self-sacrifice on the cross. This love is "poured out in our hearts by the Holy Spirit" (Romans 5:5). Pentecostals recognize that divine love flows from the Holy Spirit (Romans 15:30) just as much as divine power for witnessing. Love for God and neighbor is our response to God's love, experienced through the Spirit. Love is "fruit of the Spirit" (Galatians 5:22). Love is "in the Spirit" (Colossians 1:8). The love of God is the source of our love, and nowhere in the New Testament does it

114

say love happens without God. The Holy Spirit gives divine love, but at the same time, we are commanded to love (Romans 13:8-10). God's love is different from mere human lust, passion, or desire. God's love is holy and supremely good. What would our churches be like if we loved one another as God and Christ love us?

3. Grace

God's love and grace go hand in hand. Divine grace is God's love shown forth to the undeserving. God's grace has inclined Him to bestow blessings from the beginning of time and has been characteristic of His dealing with people throughout the ages. The Old Testament says, "Noah found grace in the eyes of the LORD" (Genesis 6:8). After the Law was given to Moses, God said, "You have also found grace in My sight" (Exodus 33:12). Divine grace is eternal and infinite. It did not begin at the coming of Christ, but it was not until the coming of Christ that grace came to its fullest expression.

The apostle John wrote, "The law was given through Moses, but grace and truth came through Jesus Christ" (1:17). Christ's self-sacrifice is grace itself (2 Corinthians 8:9). The New Testament speaks of this as a free gift (Romans 5:15). Grace is what believers are called to (Galatians 1:6) and from which they are not to fall away (5:4). Often Paul spoke of grace as being "in Christ" and he never separated it from Christ. Anywhere any person has received grace, it has been because of Christ.

Although grace came by Christ, grace did not wait until Christ took on flesh to become operative. Adam was saved by the grace of Christ. He looked forward to the coming Redeemer and believed God's promise of the Savior who would bruise the head of the serpent (Genesis 3:15).

4. Mercy

Mercy is God's love and goodness shown to those in distress and trouble and to those who are guilty. Mercy disposes God to be compassionate toward the miserable, the wretched, and wrongdoers. God is merciful, but He is also just. He has always dealt with humankind in mercy and justice. His justice is revealed in the judgment of sin. At the same time, God bestows compassion on the victims of sin. The cross of Christ is the supreme manifestation of God's justice and mercy. On the cross Jesus Christ paid the penalty for our sin and satisfied the demands of divine justice. The death of Christ was the cost to God for being merciful to the guilty. Through the cross God exercised mercy toward sinners without compromising with sin. God has always been merciful. He is the merciful One, and we are to be merciful even as God our Father (Luke 6:36).

5. Faithfulness (Truthfulness)

God is absolutely consistent. He is completely reliable and firmly constant. Never is He given to shams or to fickleness. He is faithful to His people and to His promises. All the divine attributes are consistent with one another. There is no conflict in God. God's faithfulness will never fail. Our faithfulness is the goal of His faithfulness. God gives Himself to us with the desire to call forth our faith and to undergird it. His faithfulness was manifested in the person of Jesus Christ. In the Savior we find that God does what He has promised to do and that His works are in full agreement with His words (Romans 3:3, 4; 2 Timothy 2:13). Christ himself is the sterling example of God's faithfulness (Hebrews 2:17; 3:2). When He comes to His final victory, Christ will ride forth in triumph, bearing the names *"Faithful* and *True"* (Revelation 19:11).

6. Holiness

The basic idea in holiness is that of separation and apartness. God is described as "glorious in holiness" (Exodus 15:11). This attribute sets God apart from all of His creation. He is the high and lofty One, supreme over all things and beings. There is none like our God. The attribute of holiness should not be distinguished too sharply from God's love. Holiness and love are not opposites, but in a sense they are different sides of the same coin. All that God does is done in holy love. All of God's attributes are holy. His character is the standard of holiness. "You shall be holy, for I the LORD your God am holy" (Leviticus 19:2).

The holiness of God may be viewed in two ways: (1) God stands in opposition to sin. He hates all sin and impurity. He is "of purer eyes than to behold evil" (Habakkuk 1:13). Sin degrades and destroys. God hates whatever is destructive to the spiritual life of the human race. (2) The holiness of God is His moral excellence. God is entirely free of evil and absolutely perfect. *All moral law and perfection have their basis in God's character.* The sinless work and character of Christ are the highest manifestation of God's holiness. It comes as no surprise that the saints will declare that God alone is holy (Revelation 15:4). He alone is perfect purity.

7. Justice (Righteousness)

God's justice, which is allied with His holiness, is seen in the fact that He always acts consistent with His own character. The law, especially the Ten Commandments, give expression to God's will and justice. It demands obedience and punishes transgression. In being just, God is impartial in His judgments and renders to each what is his due. The psalmist spoke of God's justice: "Righteous are You, O LORD, and upright are Your judgments" (Psalm 119:137). God deals with us without showing favoritism. From Him we receive what is just. As the psalmist says, "Righteousness and justice are the foundation of Your throne" (89:14). Speaking of how God deals with Jews and Gentiles, Paul declared, "There is no partiality with God" (Romans 2:11).

God bestows blessings of salvation, but not at the expense of justice. All people have broken the law by sinning (Romans 3:23). And God said, "The soul who sins shall die" (Ezekiel 18:4). But on the ground of Christ's merit, God rewards believers with eternal life. Blessing believers with salvation, God does not act contrary to His justice. Christ bore the penalty of death for our sins, satisfying the justice of God regarding sin and sinners. The law that demanded the death of the transgressor was satisfied. Because of the Cross, God extends His mercy to believers, sparing them the penalty of eternal death. God bestows salvation solely on the basis of grace and through faith. But there will be a judgment day, when all who are unsaved will stand before the throne of God. On that day there will be justice. Christ himself, who died in our place, will be the judge.

C. Volitional Attributes

1. Sovereign Will

God directs the events of the universe and overrules the actions of His creatures according to His perfect will. He is free to carry out His plan in every detail. Behind all that happens is His sovereign will (Psalm 115:3; Acts 2:23; Ephesians 1:5, 9, 11). Here we are faced with a profound mystery of the outworking of His will. God rules over and directs all things.

The sovereign will of God raises two pressing concerns: (1) The problem of sin. Since God is sovereign, why does He allow sin?

Could Satan have had any contact with Adam and Eve in Paradise if God had not permitted it? The only legitimate answer is that God in His sovereign wisdom has allowed sin to exist. Sin is limited and temporary. Since sin is temporary, this affirms that God is all-wise and good. And, too, He has made sin the occasion to manifest His grace and glory. (2) The issue of human freedom. Scriptures teach that we alone, and not God, are responsible for the choices we make. God has given us freedom to choose either good or evil. Freedom is not contrary to but a fulfillment of God's will. God wills that we be free moral agents, though He remains sovereign Lord. God limits Himself to make room for our freedom and responsibility. An earthly king may have absolute authority over his people, but he may limit his control by giving them certain rights and privileges. The sovereign God has done something like that. God has created us not to be as robots but as people endowed with freedom of choice.

The Scriptures place human freedom and responsibility alongside the absolute rule of God. For example, the death of Jesus Christ was part of the plan of the sovereign God, but that in no way relieved the lawless men who crucified Him of responsibility for His death (Acts 2:23). God controls the affairs of this world in the context of human freedom. Even when individuals misuse freedom and do wrong, God has a way of using it to accomplish His plan for this world. Joseph's brothers sold Him into Egypt, but God used that cruel deed to keep His people alive when a famine struck Canaan (Genesis 50:20).

2. Sovereign Power (Omnipotence)

This attribute expresses the perfect ability of God to do what He wills. Scripture asserts this truth in a variety of ways.

God is *El Shaddai* (Genesis 17:1). God is "the King of kings and Lord of lords" (1 Timothy 6:15). He is "the Lord God Omnipotent" (Revelation 19:6). Nothing is impossible with God (Luke 1:37). Scripture makes it clear that when He spoke, it was done (Genesis 1:3). So the God who reveals Himself as the God of love and holiness shows Himself as the Almighty. He is the God who has done mighty miracles and wonders for His people.

Rightly understood, the omnipotence of God is not a threat but a comfort to Christians. However, it stands in contrast to human and logical ideas of having all power. In the Crucifixion the Son of God appeared to be weak and defeated by His enemies, but there was never a greater manifestation of divine omnipotence than through the cross of Christ. According to human reason the crucified Jesus suffered defeat at the hands of His enemies. But through that ignominious event, Almighty God disarmed evil powers and principalities and triumphed over them (Colossians 2:15). By surrendering Himself to death, the Son of God manifested the incomparable character of divine omnipotence and provided salvation for us.

Attributes Not Discernible in Humankind
Some divine attributes are in some degree reflected in humankind, but other attributes are not found in human beings. A number of these can be identified.

A. Self-existence (Aseity, Independence)
The life of God has neither beginning nor end. To use the language of adoration, God is "from everlasting to everlasting" (Psalm 90:2). All creatures and created things had a beginning, but not God. He is not dependent for His existence on anything outside of Himself. He is self-existent. Jesus spoke of the Father

as having "life in Himself" (John 5:26). None of God's creatures have life in themselves; all life is a gift of God. God is described as not needing "anything, since He gives to all life, breath, and all things" (Acts 17:25). His interest in us arises from His love and good pleasure, not from need. So God is self-sufficient in His being and works. But He does use means outside of Himself to accomplish His purpose. For example, so that souls may be saved and the church edified, God has called believers in Christ to make the gospel known to the world.

B. Eternity

God exists above time and is unaffected by it. The prophet Isaiah described Him as "the High and Lofty One who inhabits eternity" (57:15). That is, God is not only exalted but He exists above time. To "inhabit" or "dwell in" eternity does not point to some place where God lives but to God's existence above the limitations of time. Scripture speaks of the "King eternal" (1 Timothy 1:17) and of the One whose "years will have no end" (Psalm 102:27). Of course, it is difficult for us to grasp the eternity of God because our present existence is within the limits of time. Each of us had a beginning, but God is without beginning. Our mortal existence will end in death, but God is without end. For us there is past, present, and future— but not for God. He transcends time, so that past, present, and future are now. He created time, placed it under His rule, and acts within time as He wills.

Time is meaningful to God, for in the fullness of time He sent His Son (Galatians 4:4). God's saving work in Christ took place in history. Jesus Christ died and rose from the dead in the first century. Because the eternal God has involved Himself in time on our behalf, "Behold, now is the accepted time; behold, now is

121

the day of salvation" (2 Corinthians 6:2). The God of eternity has entered into our world and provides through His Son salvation for us.

C. Omnipresence

The attribute of eternity reminds us that God is Lord over time. He also is Lord over space. Omnipresence means that He is not limited by space and thus He is present everywhere at once. In Psalm 139 David declared that God is present in all the universe. David inquired, "Where can I go from Your Spirit? Or where can I flee from Your presence?" (v. 7). These questions are rhetorical, and so he answers, "If I ascend into heaven, You are there; if I make my bed in hell [sheol], behold, You are there. If I take the wings of the morning, and dwell in the uttermost parts of the sea, even there Your hand shall lead me" (vv. 8-10). As his answer indicates, David had no desire to flee from God's presence, for God is everywhere—not only in this world but in all realms of life we may inhabit.

None of us can hide from God, whether it is in heaven, earth, or hell. "'Do I not fill heaven and earth?' says the LORD" (Jeremiah 23:24). "He is not far from each one of us; for in Him we live and move and have our being" (Acts 17:27, 28). God sees, hears, and knows everything because He is present everywhere to see, hear, and know everything. Where two or three believers are gathered in the Lord's name, He is present (Matthew 18:20). Christ dwells in our hearts (Ephesians 3:17) and has promised to be with us to the end of the age (Matthew 28:20).

Equally as certain is that God's revelation in Christ occurred in time and space. God manifested Himself at a definite place, for in Christ "dwells all the fullness of the Godhead bodily" (Colossians 2:9). The saving work of God in Christ was local and spatial. God came from His own place, which the Bible describes as heaven. But though heaven is not able to contain Him (1 Kings 8:27), it has been made by Him as has the earth. God, who is present in all His creation, took up His abode on the earth in Jesus Christ. Since His ascension, Christ sits at the right hand of God (Colossians 3:1). He is there, and He is with us. He dwells in the place called heaven and in our hearts. In heaven we have our citizenship, and from it "we also eagerly wait for the Savior, the Lord Jesus Christ" (Philippines 3:20). The omnipresent God has revealed Himself at a specific time and place and will do so again at the return of His Son. In the meantime, we can worship God and commune with Him anywhere and at any time, since He is present everywhere. The doctrine of God's omnipresence assures us that He is present to help us.

D. Immutability

The God of the Bible is One who does not change. This means that God is consistently good, He is constantly faithful to His promises, and He is absolutely dependable. God will never be any better than He is now, because He is the perfection of goodness. He will never be any holier than He is now, because He is the essence of holiness. God's attitude toward sin is the same as the day He drove Adam and Eve out of the Garden of Eden. As God has always been, He is receptive to faith and love.

God moves and acts, but He is changeless (Malachi 3:6). All other things change, but God is "the Father of lights, with whom there is no variation or shadow of turning" (James 1:17). Likewise Christ is declared to be "the same yesterday, today, and forever" (Hebrews 13:8). Whether the Father, the Son, or the Holy Spirit, God does not change. However, Scripture says that

God repents and changes His mind. Some scholars have insisted that God does not really change His mind. But to say that assumes that what Scripture affirms about God does not mean what it says. How can we explain the statements about God's grief and repentance without explaining them away?

There is no change in God's character, nature, purpose, and promises. But how should divine immutability be understood in light of 1 Samuel 15:11, where God said, "It repented me that I have set up Saul to be king" (KJV). After Samuel told Saul that God would take the kingdom from him and give it to David, he said, "The Strength of Israel will not lie nor repent" (15:29, KJV). The repentance of God does not deny His unchanging nature, but it expresses His faithfulness and consistency in meeting any conditions that may arise. To remain faithful to His promise, God took the kingdom from Saul and gave it to David. Saul's failures threatened God's Word and promise (1 Samuel 12:13-15).

When taken in its biblical context, the repentance of God means that He deals faithfully with situations so that His unchangeable purpose will prevail.

The Bible points consistently to God's concern about what happens on the earth. Behind the idea "God repents" is that He cares for men and women. At the center of the faith of Pentecostals is the conviction that God does respond to what we do and enters into our experiences. He draws near to us and discloses Himself as we draw near to Him. He hears prayer and shows that He is concerned about what ascends to Him from the world. So God is moved by what happens on the earth and changes His behavior to accomplish His unchanging purpose. Yet God Himself does not change. There is no change in His character, purpose, and motives for action. In contrast to this world of constant change and instability, God is absolutely faithful and dependable. He is the Rock of our salvation, our strength and stability.

Conclusion

The way each attribute has been presented as a distinct characteristic of God should not be taken to mean that an attribute is just a part of His being. Each attribute describes God as He is in His total being. God is holy and all-powerful in His total being. God is not bound by any of the limitations of time and space as they apply to us. The attributes point to the self-existent and self-revealing God. As Scripture sets forth, God in Christ has entered into our experiences of pain, sorrow, and joy. God's attributes show Him to be truthful, faithful, and merciful. They show Him to be the God of grace, patience, constancy, wisdom, justice, and goodness. For these glorious characteristics He is eternally worthy to be praised, loved, and served with Pentecostal fervor and devotion.

Chapter 9

THE HOLY TRINITY

At the very center of the Christian message stands a profound mystery: the one God exists in three persons: Father, Son, and Holy Spirit. The church has used for a long time the expression "three persons in the one Godhead." *The idea that God exists in three persons is known as the doctrine of the Trinity. The blessed Trinity is God the Father, God the Son, and God the Holy Spirit.* "So the Father is God; the Son is God; and the Holy Ghost is God. And yet there are not three gods but one God" (Athanasian Creed).

The doctrine of the Trinity stresses the perfect fellowship and relationship within the triune God. The three persons of the Godhead enjoy the closest ties of love and common purpose. The personal relationship within the Trinity has special significance for the Pentecostal experience. The Holy Spirit, for example, has endued the Pentecostal believer with power for service consistent with the commissioning of Jesus Christ, God's Son (see Luke 3:21, 22; 4:1, 18, 19). As Jesus Christ was called by God the Father and anointed with the power of the Holy Spirit, Pentecostal believers have been called of God and endued with the power of the Holy Spirit. As the anointing of Jesus was an example of the perfect relationship of the Father, the Son, and the Holy Spirit, so is the Pentecostals' experience. This fact became clear in the outpouring of the Holy Spirit as told in Acts 2. The disciples' experience of the Holy Spirit on that occasion flowed from the victorious Christ; but the Holy Spirit, whom He gave, had been promised by the Father (Acts 2:33). At the very heart of the Pentecostal experience is the work of the triune God. He is always present in all of His works.

That God exists only by existing as Father, Son, and Holy Spirit provides the foundation for Pentecostal experience and worship. But the doctrine of the Trinity cannot be grasped by mere human understanding. Only by the Holy Spirit can we discern the deep things of God (1 Corinthians 2:10-14). The Holy Spirit can help our understanding to penetrate the veil of the Holy of Holies and accept God's gracious disclosure of Himself as one being existing in three persons. The Scriptures are the ground of our faith, and we turn to them as the basis of our understanding of the mystery of the Trinity.

The One God

The Bible affirms that God is one. In the Old Testament the fundamental confession of faith is "Hear, O Israel: The LORD our God, the LORD is one!" (Deuteronomy 6:4). This confession strongly expresses the unity of God. The Old Testament teaches that there is a God and this God is one. So whatever we say about God's existing in three persons, the unity of God must also be emphasized. His unity is basic and the starting point of our faith. Our concern in dealing with the doctrine of the Trinity is not to question the unity of God but to emphasize and preserve it.

There is no need for us to give lengthy proofs that the Bible testifies there is one God. Over against the pagan world with its many gods, the Old Testament proclaims that there is no God but Jehovah. The unity of God could very well summarize the message of the prophets (Deuteronomy 4:35; 2 Kings 19:15; Jeremiah 2:11). The prophet Isaiah vigorously declared, speaking for God, "I am the LORD, that is My name; and My glory I will not give to another" (42:8).

The New Testament is just as emphatic. Jesus reaffirmed the fundamental article of faith in the Old Testament when He said, "Hear, O Israel, the LORD our God, the LORD is one" (Mark 12:29). The apostle Paul assumed that his readers understood that God is one (1 Corinthians 8:4-6). He also spoke of "one God and Father of all" (Ephesians 4:6). There are powerful repetitions of this confession throughout the New Testament (John 17:3; Romans 3:30; 1 Timothy 2:5; Jude 25). We need only to read these passages to recognize the boldness of the biblical testimony to the one and only God.

The doctrine of the unity of God is part of the gospel, the joyful news, and has great practical significance for us. First, worship offered to various gods makes a center of devotion impossible. To worship the one and only God focuses our devotion on Him alone. According to Deuteronomy 6:5, "You shall love the LORD your God with all your heart, with all your soul, and with all your might." All worship is to be rendered to God and only to Him. Second, God as one has a practical bearing also on our sense of personal and community unity. Our relationships and activities are many, but the one LORD God can unify and integrate all of life with its numerous relationships and activities. He gives life meaning, direction, and focus that it would not have otherwise. The same can be said of His relation to the Christian community. The unity of God makes for unity in the church by holding the people of God together. Their relationship with the one God is the powerful bond of their fellowship and unity. Hence, God's unity is the basis of Christian unity. There is "one God and Father of all, who is above all, and through all, and in you all" (Ephesians 4:6). Thus the unity of God has practical significance for all of life and Christian experience.

The One God in Three Persons

The Bible repeatedly tells that there is only one God. But as the Scripture unfolds, it becomes increasingly clear that God exists in three persons. The divine attributes and the fact of the Trinity point to an immensely rich diversity of existence in the unity of God. God is one, but the New Testament expresses a specific distinction in the Godhead by identifying three persons. They are identified as Father, Son, and Holy Spirit.

A. Witness of the Old Testament

In the Old Testament some evidence points in the direction of the Trinity. The prophet Isaiah implied that God is more than one person. He said, "And now the Lord GOD and His Spirit have sent Me" (48:16). The same prophet said that Israel "rebelled and grieved His Holy Spirit" (63:10). And there are other such references to the Spirit of God as One by whom God spoke and acted in the world (Genesis 1:2; Job 33:4; Micah 3:8; Zechariah 7:12). There are also such expressions as "Who will go for Us?" (Isaiah 6:8) and "Let Us make man in Our image, according to Our likeness" (Genesis 1:26). That God is more than one person is also implied by the divine name *Elohim*. "In the beginning God [*Elohim*] created . . ." (Genesis 1:1). *Elohim* is plural. Though it does not specifically describe God the Trinity, the plurality and unity of God is suggested by the name *Elohim*.

In Isaiah's vision of the LORD, the threefold utterance of the seraphim, "Holy, holy, holy," (6:3), may be taken as pointing to the three persons of the Godhead. An even clearer anticipation of the doctrine of the Trinity may be seen in "the Angel of the LORD." This angel appeared to Moses in the burning bush and said, "I am the God of your father—the God of Abraham, the God of Isaac, and the God of Jacob" (Exodus 3:6). He identified himself as God, but he was also distinguished from God (Genesis 16:11). Jacob called this angel the redeemer from all evil: "the God who has fed me all my life . . . the Angel who has redeemed me from all evil" (Genesis 48:15, 16).

Of all the Old Testament scriptures that may hint at the Trinity, one already mentioned may be the most significant: "And now the Lord GOD and His Spirit have sent Me" (Isaiah 48:16). If these are to be taken as the words of the Messiah, they mean that the Spirit and the Father sent the Son (cf. Luke 4:1, 14, 18). So, in the Old Testament there are intimations of the plurality of God and even some indications that this plurality is the Trinity.

B. Witness of the New Testament

The burden of the Old Testament is the unity of God, but in the New Testament the overwhelming evidence is that God exists in three persons.

1. The Trinitarian Pattern

All three persons of the Godhead are mentioned in relation

to the baptism of Jesus. On that occasion the Holy Spirit descended upon Jesus, the Son, and the Father spoke His approval of the Son (Matthew 3:16, 17). Those who become disciples of Jesus are to be baptized in the name of the Father, the Son, and the Holy Spirit (28:19). The apostolic benediction speaks of the grace of Christ, the love of God, and the communion of the Holy Spirit (2 Corinthians 13:14). The people of God have access through Christ by the one Spirit to the Father (Ephesians 2:18). Reference is made to God's people being chosen by the Father and sanctified by the Spirit for obedience to Jesus Christ (1 Peter 1:2). The trinitarian pattern also appears in this exhortation: "Praying in the Holy Spirit, keep yourselves in the love of God, looking for the mercy of our Lord Jesus Christ" (Jude 20, 21).

The reality of the Holy Trinity is evident in the manifestation of spiritual gifts. There are varieties of ministries, but they proceed from the same Spirit. There are varieties of ministries, but it is the same Lord (Christ) to whom ultimately all service is rendered. There are many operations of the gifts, but the same God (Father) works in every believer (1 Corinthians 12:4-6).

The outpouring of the Holy Spirit at Pentecost pointed clearly to the Trinity (Acts 2:1-33). The fullness of the Spirit was the "promise of the Father." Yet God's Son, the exalted Christ, having received from the Father the promised Holy Spirit, sent the Spirit forth to His followers. However, the Pentecostal manifestation also issued from the person of the Spirit. He gave the utterance of tongues, filled worshipers, and declared the great works of God through them (2:3, 4, 11). All the spiritual manifestations seen and heard at Pentecost flowed from the victorious Christ; but the promised Holy Spirit, whom He gave and continues to give, Christ received from the Father (2:33).

Another example of the Trinity is seen in the experience of Stephen. Before a mob stoned him, Stephen, full of the Holy

Spirit, looked into heaven and saw the Lord Jesus standing at the right hand of God the Father (7:55). Many other passages in the New Testament speak of the three persons. Among these are Romans 15:16, 30; 2 Corinthians 1:21, 22; Ephesians 2:18. So the New Testament reveals God to us as Father, Son, and Holy Spirit. God is one but at the same time triune.

2. Three Distinct Persons of the Godhead

Christians believe that the one God exists in three persons: Father, Son, and Holy Spirit. The Scriptures clearly teach that the Father is God. Jesus frequently spoke about God the Father. His disclosure of God sprang directly from His knowledge of God as *His* Father. The Father loves the Son and confers all authority on Him (John 3:35; 5:17-45). Jesus portrayed God's fatherly care in many of the parables. Through their trust in Jesus the disciples came to experience the care of the heavenly Father and committed themselves to His will. More and more they became caught up in the reality of God as their Father.

Repeatedly the New Testament bears witness that God is the Father. He is described as "the Father of glory" (Ephesians 1:17) and "the God and Father of our Lord Jesus Christ" (1:3). The fatherhood of God is the basis for family relationships among people, and especially of the family of believers (3:14, 15). The Holy Spirit testifies to the heart of believers that God is the Father: "And because you are sons, God has sent forth the Spirit of His Son into your hearts, crying out, 'Abba, Father!'" (Galatians 4:6). So the inner witness of the Holy Spirit enables believers to come to an intimate knowledge of God as Father.

As it applies to God, we must not think of *Father* as only a title. Father signifies a real relationship. A person becomes a father by begetting another. In the New Testament, *Father* has a new meaning, which is seen in two ways: (1) God's relationship with Christ and (2) God's relationship with believers. The Father's relationship with Christ is unique because it is eternal (John 17:1-5). God has forever been the Father of the Lord Jesus Christ. Jesus is the incomparable Son of God. But God is also the Father of believers. Since believers are "born again" and adopted into God's family, they (we) are children of "God our Father" (Romans 1:7). So then, God the Father is more than a personal designation for God. His fatherhood has to do with His relationship with Jesus Christ and with all who have received life through Him.

The Father is God, but the New Testament declares His Son is also God. In Scripture, God the Father and Jesus the Son are placed side by side so that it becomes clear they are coequal. A typical apostolic salutation is pronounced with the words "Grace to you and peace from God the Father and our Lord Jesus Christ" (Galatians 1:3). In addition to being linked with the Father on equal terms, Jesus did what only God can do. He spoke with divine authority, even with more authority than Moses (Matthew 19:3-9). He forgave sins (9:2). The authority and power to forgive sins belongs to God alone. It is not surprising that the Pharisees charged Jesus with blasphemy when He claimed to do what only God can do (Luke 5:20, 21). The entire biblical message of redemption rests on the claim that deliverance from sin belongs to God alone.

In so many ways Scriptures declare Jesus to be God. Frequently He is called "the Son of God" (Mark 1:1, 11; Romans 1:4; Galatians 4:4). The term *Son of God* is a title of deity. The Sanhedrin condemned Jesus because He claimed to be God, the Son of God (Matthew 26:63-65; John 19:7). Jesus Christ is called the Word of God: "In the beginning was the Word . . . and the Word was God" (John 1:1). The full deity of the Son is declared in the statement "The Word was God." And there are other passages where the term God is directly used of Jesus. For example, "Christ came, who is over all, the eternally blessed God" (Romans 9:5) and "the righteousness of our God and Savior Jesus Christ" (2 Peter 1:1). The words "over all" and "God and Savior" clearly teach that Jesus Christ is God.

Moreover, Jesus Christ is honored and worshiped as God. Thomas so worshiped Jesus when he exclaimed, "My Lord and my God!" (John 20:28); and Stephen did likewise when "calling on God," he said, "Lord Jesus, receive my spirit" (Acts 7:59). After the believers were filled with the Spirit at Pentecost, Peter proclaimed that "God has made this Jesus, whom you [the Jews] crucified, both Lord and Christ" (Acts 2:36). This title LORD ascribed to Jesus clearly identified Him with Jehovah and attributed to Him the same authority (see Matthew 3:3 and Isaiah 40:3). So the early believers confessed Jesus as Lord, who is "far above all principality and power and might and dominion, and every name that is named, not only in this age but also in that which is to come" (Ephesians 1:21).

The understanding of Christ as God arose out of revelation and personal experience. The first Christians were Jews, that is, people who believed in the one God. Yet they became aware that Christ was not just a man sent from God, or a prophet, or an angel. As they associated with Him, they realized that though He was truly human, He also was God. They came to know Him personally as their Savior. They confessed Him as Lord and worshiped Him (Matthew 14:33; Luke 5:8). He was the very Son of God—Immanuel, "God with us." The Bible declares Jesus Christ to be God; but like the first believers, many people today through personal experience have found Him to be both God and Savior.

Scripture places the Holy Spirit on equal footing with the Father and the Son. He is not merely a divine influence but a divine person, who is distinct from the Father and the Son. He is also called "the Spirit of Jesus Christ." Throughout the New Testament all of the titles of the Spirit are gathered up in the expression "the Holy Spirit," and they indicate the essential unity of the Godhead.

Many scriptures compel us to regard the Holy Spirit as God, coequal with the Father and Son. These same scriptures make it clear that we are to understand the Spirit is a person. He performs personal acts such as teaching (John 14:26), commissioning (Acts 13:2), guiding (Acts 16:6), and interceding (Romans 8:26). He is affected in personal ways. He can be blasphemed (Matthew 12:31, 32) and grieved (Ephesians 4:30). He has intelligence—"the Spirit searches all things, yes, the deep things of God" (1 Corinthians 2:10). He has will—the Spirit distributes spiritual gifts "to each one individually as He wills" (12:11). The Holy Spirit is identified as God. When Ananias lied to the Holy Spirit, Peter declared, "You have not lied to men but to God" (Acts 5:3, 4). In lying to the person of the Holy Spirit, Ananias lied to God.

It should be noted that for the early believers the Holy Spirit was an experiential reality. Their new awareness of the Holy Spirit came not only from their initial Pentecostal experience but from His daily guidance and fellowship and from the many miraculous manifestations of His power. Many believers were described as "full of the Holy Spirit" (Acts 6:3, 5; 7:55; 11:24). The Spirit directed the entire mission of the church. The Jerusalem Council could say, "It seemed good to the Holy Spirit, and to us" (15:28). The Spirit caused missionaries to change their proposed route for travel in Asia (16:6-8). The prophet Agabus declared, "Thus says the Holy Spirit" (21:11).

The New Testament Christians' experience of the Holy Spirit never became a mere experience of the past. He continued to speak and to act in their midst. He was a dynamic, ever-present reality, and the early Christians knew He was God. In the present-day outpouring of the Spirit, many believers have also experienced the Holy Spirit as God. Their hearts have been warmed by this fresh outpouring of the Spirit, and through the Spirit they have experienced God's powerful personal presence and His mighty works in their midst.

The Trinity in Unity

God is a unified being. There is not just one but three persons in the Godhead. There is the Father who is the Creator and source of all things. There is the Son who redeems us. There is the Holy Spirit who regenerates, sanctifies, and fills us with His power. Each has His own identity. The distinct identity of each was evident at the baptism of Jesus. The Son of God was standing in the Jordan. He was anointed by the Holy Spirit, who came upon Him in the form of a dove, and the Father spoke from heaven (Luke 3:21, 22).

The reality of the personal distinction of each person of the Godhead can be seen in a number of ways. For example, the Son, not the Father nor the Spirit, became flesh (John 1:14). The Son, not the Father nor the Spirit, suffered on the cross (Romans 5:8-11). The Son, not the Father nor the Holy Spirit, ascended into heaven (Acts 1:11). The Son will return in power and glory to put all enemies under His feet and to deliver the Kingdom to God the Father (1 Corinthians 15:24, 25). The Lord Jesus said He would send the Spirit from the Father (John 15:26) and that the Spirit would bear witness not of Himself but of Christ (16:13). The Holy Spirit did not beget the Son, but the Father from all eternity did (1:14, 18). The Spirit is not only called "the Spirit of the Father" but also "the Spirit of the Son" (Galatians 4:6).

In this life we are not able to fathom fully the relations of the triune God. But Scriptures affirm that God knows nothing of being alone. The Father, the Son, and the Holy Spirit have always been in perfect communion and fellowship with one another. Mutual love has characterized the fellowship of the eternal Father, the eternal Son, and the eternal Spirit. Scripture places the Father in the forefront in the work of creation, the Son in the forefront in the work of redemption, and the Holy Spirit in the forefront in the work of sanctification and equipping believers to be witnesses of Christ. Yet, in all these works the triune God fully participates. The Father, the Son, and the Holy Spirit redeem sinners. The Father, the Son, and the Holy Spirit sanctify and equip believers as witnesses. Each of the divine persons cooperates and participates in all the activities of the Godhead. So there is no work of the Father that is not the work of the Son and the Holy Spirit. All three work together as one. What the Father does, the Son and the Holy Spirit also do.

Another way to describe the unity of the Trinity is that each person in the Godhead has all divine perfections. The Son and the Holy Spirit have the same attributes as the Father. The Father is infinite, eternal, unchangeable, all-knowing, and all-powerful. The same can be said of the Son and the Holy Spirit. Each person is equal with the other. They are equally divine, eternal, and unchangeable. They are equal in power, equal in glory, and equal in might. They are entitled to the same worship, the same devotion, and the same reverence and trust. When we worship the Son or the Holy Spirit, we neither worship one who is less than God nor only part of God. To adore the Son is to adore the Father and the Holy Spirit. If we look to the Holy Spirit for power to witness and to exercise spiritual gifts, we rely on the Father and the Son also. When we serve the Father, we serve also the Son and the Holy Spirit. They are not three masters but only one—one God in three persons.

Some False Explanations

Various attempts have been made to explain the Trinity. The problem has been to maintain the biblical idea of only one God but at the same time recognize God as Father, Son, and Holy Spirit. Some interpretations have proved to be inadequate in light of Scripture. Among the false interpretations is the view that Jesus Christ was a mere man who was filled with God's Spirit so He could perform miracles. Another version is that Christ was only an exalted creature and therefore not equal with the Father. Similar erroneous views of the Holy Spirit have been advocated. Some who deny the deity of the Holy Spirit see Him as a mere impersonal power or influence.

Today there are two false views of God (modalism and tritheism) that continue to have great influence. Both of these views have been condemned as heresy by the church. Because either may be embraced due to a lack of understanding, a brief discussion of each is in order.

A. Modalism

This view insists that God is only one person and that the one divine person has manifested Himself in three modes or three ways. That is, God plays three roles. At one time God plays the role of the Father, at another time He plays the role of the Son, and at still another time He manifests Himself as the Holy Spirit. To illustrate this view: I am a father, a taxpayer, and a teacher. I play these three different roles at different times, but I am only one person. According to modalism the one divine person does likewise. The Father, Son, and Holy Spirit are modes through which God reveals Himself and accomplishes His purposes. He assumes different forms and plays different roles. When He is the Creator and the Lawgiver, He reveals

Himself as the Father. When He is the Redeemer and the Spirit-baptizer, He reveals Himself as the Son. When He is the life-giver, He reveals Himself as the Holy Spirit. So modalism teaches that God wears three different masks—sometimes the mask of the Father, at other times the mask of the Son, and on some occasions the mask of the Holy Spirit. Modalism is proven wrong by biblical teaching regarding the personal distinctions in the Godhead.

B. Tritheism

Modalism emphasizes the unity of God to the exclusion of the Trinity. On the other hand, tritheism emphasizes the distinctiveness of the Father, the Son, and the Holy Spirit to the point of denying the essential unity of God. This view separates the three persons and teaches that there are three different Gods. The idea of three Gods corresponds to that of three players sitting on the bench in a football game. The Father goes out and plays until He is tired. Then He sends the Son, and He goes out and plays for a while. When He gets tired, He comes back and sends the Holy Spirit into the game. This analogy may help us to understand tritheism, for it proposes that there are three Gods who are on the same team. The Father is the first God, the second God is the Son, and the third God is the Holy Spirit. But the Bible says there is only one God. The doctrine of the Trinity (one God who exists in three persons) does not deny the unity of God, but tritheism does. Tritheism is not in accord with Scripture.

The Trinitarian Way of Life

The full significance of the Trinity makes it more than a doctrine. It is a way of life. From all eternity the blessed Trinity (Father, Son, and Holy Spirit) have been communing with one another and enjoying one another's fellowship. In New Testament times God revealed Himself fully in Jesus Christ. Those who had faith in Christ came to see Him as the revelation of God and realized that He shared the very nature of God. Jesus Himself said that He came from God, and He spoke of God in a unique personal way as His Father (Matthew 11:25-27). The church recognized Jesus as the Son of God (Acts 9:20; Romans 1:3, 4) and worshiped Him as Lord (Romans 10:9-13). Jesus spoke of sending "another Helper" (John 14:16), the Holy Spirit, from the Father. The earliest Christians experienced the Holy Spirit as promised by Jesus. More than that, they actually had fellowship with the blessed Trinity, and their lives were enriched by the worship of the triune God. The unity and life of the Father, Son, and Holy Spirit became the very basis of the first believers' lives and fellowship with one another. Love binds together believers so that they live in the unity of the body of Christ (Colossians 3:14). Such community flows from believers' being joined to the Father, the Son, and the Holy Spirit, who have perfect fellowship among themselves in the Godhead. The foundation of our life in Christ and our Pentecostal experience and worship is the blessed Trinity.

To conclude on a devotional note, by the Holy Spirit we are made partakers of Christ and joint heirs with Christ. By the same Spirit we cry "Abba, Father" and give praise to the Father, the Son, and the Holy Spirit—one God, blessed forever.

Glory be to the Father
And to the Son,
And to the Holy Ghost;
As it was in the beginning,
Is now,
And ever shall be,
World without end, Amen.

Part Three:
DOCTRINE
OF
CREATION

Chapter 10

THE CREATOR AND HIS CREATION

The Bible from Genesis to Revelation affirms that God created the world. The universe is not self-existent; for as the first chapter of Genesis teaches, God is the source and the Creator of it. The living God said, "Let there be . . ." and there was. As great and magnificent as His creation is, the Creator is far greater than the universe. God inhabits eternity, and the earth is like a mere footstool to Him (Isaiah 57:15; 66:1). Creation may be characterized as a mystery, but neither God nor Creation is essentially incomprehensible in light of divine revelation in the Scriptures.

The Pentecostal view of Creation is the biblical view; but to appreciate adequately the true significance of Creation, Pentecostals believe the Holy Spirit must enlighten our inward eye to what has been revealed in God's Word. The Bible and the God of the Bible are the authorities for our belief in Creation. Pentecostals realize that the biblical writers made no attempt to describe the origin of the universe in scientific language. Their purpose was not to instruct in the modern science of astronomy or biology but to declare the ultimate origin and final destiny of the universe.

God the Creator

The Bible begins with God as the Creator. Its opening statement is "In the beginning God created the heavens and the earth" (Genesis 1:1). The study of the biblical doctrine of Creation must begin with God and what He has revealed in Scripture. Consequently, the truth of Creation belongs to the arena of revelation and faith. It is important to recall the words of Hebrews 11:3: "By faith we understand that the worlds were framed by the word of God." Only with eyes of faith illuminated by the Spirit can we truly grasp the creation of all things by the living God. As Christians we have experienced the miracle of the new creation by faith in Christ (2 Corinthians 5:17). By the same faith we understand that all creation came forth from God and His word. The Bible tells three things about God that indicate how we are to understand His creation and our place in it.

A. In the Beginning God Created

What this means is that the world had a beginning and its beginning was God. The Creation had its foundation and origin in the personal God alone. "By the word of the Lord the heavens were made, and all the host of them by the breath of His mouth. . . . For He spoke, and it was done; He commanded, and it stood fast" (Psalm 33:6, 9). The Bible makes no attempt to date the beginning. The only thing we can say is that at the beginning of time God created the world. The eternal God brought the world from nonexistence into existence. When we behold at every turn the many forms of life and nature in its beauty, the question may be "Who made all this?" No way can this be adequately answered without speaking about the wonder of God's creative work and His continual care of the universe.

A significant verse of Scripture may be noted here. Thinking of the creative power of God, Paul described God as the One "who gives life to the dead and calls those things which do not exist as though they did" (Romans 4:17). The God who raises the dead to life is the God who gave existence to the universe. The creation of the heavens and earth stand at the beginning, but the new heaven and earth stand at the end (Revelation 21:1). The final creative work of God will not only involve the renewal of the heaven and earth but the resurrection of His people and completion of their salvation.

It is important to realize that the biblical account of Creation cannot be understood by the natural mind. The eyes of faith are required for a true understanding not only of the new creation in Christ but also of Creation at the beginning. Therefore an unbeliever can have little success in perceiving the real meaning of the doctrine of Creation. The unbeliever does not understand the things of the Spirit of God "because they are spiritually discerned" (1 Corinthians 2:14). Without faith, energized by the Holy Spirit, the Bible remains essentially a closed book. That is just as true of the biblical account of Creation as other teachings of Scripture.

B. God Created the Universe out of Nothing

The Creator did not begin with previously existing material and from it make the universe. Rather, the Bible emphatically teaches that God created the universe out of nothing (ex nihilo). "In the beginning God created the heavens and the earth" (Genesis 1:1). The word *created* (Hebrew, *bara*) appears also in

Genesis 1:27 with respect to the creation of Adam and is used in the Bible only of God's unique and unprecedented activity. God's creative work has no close human parallel. Our creative work involves working with materials that are already in existence. A potter makes a vessel out of clay, and a carpenter makes a chair out of wood. With God it is different. We create (make things) out of what God has given, but God created the universe out of nothing. He created the materials as well as gave them distinct forms. Consequently the creative activity of God is distinctively unique.

The expression "created out of nothing" does not appear in the Bible, but this doctrine has its basis in Scripture (Psalm 33:9; Romans 4:17). Hebrews 11:3 offers the most conclusive support: "The worlds were framed by the word of God, so that the things which are seen were not made of things which are visible." There is no attempt to explain how this happened. The only explanation the Bible gives is that the world came into existence by the sheer power of God's word. God spoke and it was done (Psalm 33:9). So the creation of the material world was an absolute origination of God—that is, it was totally new, having been created out of no preexisting material.

C. God Created for His Glory and for Our Sake

Creation is the work of the magnificent power of God. But behind creation stands not only an all-powerful but also a loving God. God willed to have a world through which He could manifest His glory and communicate His love to us. Creation is an arena where we see the manifestation of God's greatness and majesty. The psalmist sang of the heavens' declaring the glory of God (19:1). The angels around the throne of God cry out, "Holy, holy, holy is the LORD of hosts; the whole earth is full of His glory!" (Isaiah 6:3). The whole of creation's testimony is designed to bring glory to the Creator. If we do not see the glory of God as the psalmist and the angels, it may be because we are focused on the dreadful consequences of sin and evil in God's good creation.

God wills to manifest His glory. He has shown His glory not only by His unlimited power but also by His goodness to us. The powerful Creator has manifested His greatness in the world not simply for the purpose of displaying His perfections; His aim has been to promote our welfare and happiness. His appointment of a definite order in creation (natural laws and social and moral laws) testifies of this truth. The same God who in Christ came into the world to express His goodness and love to us is the Creator. The God who created all things is the God who saves.

The recognition of God's glory in His works should prompt us, as part of His creation, to glorify Him. Indeed He is worthy to receive our grateful praise and thanksgiving. The song the elders sing around the throne of God is an appropriate response to the Creator of heaven and earth: "You are worthy, O Lord, to receive glory and honor and power; for You created all things, and by Your will they exist and were created" (Revelation 4:11). Such a response fulfills the purpose of all creation to glorify God. And, too, by offering grateful praise we experience His blessing and find meaning for our lives in the world.

The Trinity and Creation

When we look at Scripture, we note that God the Father is closely linked with the work of Creation. But the Son and the Holy Spirit also participated. We think of God the Father as the ultimate author of Creation, but because of the essential unity of the Trinity, the Son and the Holy Spirit had an active part in Creation. It is in keeping with the Bible to ascribe the work of Creation to the three persons of the Godhead. Yet we may describe the special functions and work of each of the persons of the Trinity insofar as Scripture does.

A. Work of the Father in Creation

In the Old Testament God is not frequently referred to as *Father*. However, two Old Testament passages do identify the Creator as Father: "Is He not your Father, who bought you? Has He not made you and established you?" (Deuteronomy 32:6). "Have we not all one Father? Has not one God created us?" (Malachi 2:10). The New Testament says, "For us there is only one God, the Father" (1 Corinthians 8:6) and "All things are from God" (11:12; cf. Romans 11:36).

Thus the Bible lays emphasis on the fact that God the Father created the heavens and the earth. The Father is peculiarly the Creator, the originator, and the founder of the universe. "He has made the earth by His power; He has established the world by His wisdom, and stretched out the heaven by His understanding" (Jeremiah 51:15). God spoke and the world came into existence. It did not originate from some impersonal force but from One who is Father. The term *Father* indicates that God is One who cares for creation and is concerned about all of His creatures. He recognizes creation as His own and rightly entitled to His care. Fatherlike, He intends good for all He created and faithfully seeks the general well-being of the world and its inhabitants.

B. Work of the Son in Creation

God the Son was the agent in Creation. Through the Son,

the eternal Word, God created the heavens and earth. The whole account of Creation in Genesis 1 is focused upon the word of God. Each deed of Creation is accomplished by His word. The creative work of God's word is not only seen in the narrative of Genesis 1, where the phrase "God said . . . and it was so" constantly recurs, but the psalmist declared, "By the word of the LORD the heavens were made, and all the host of them by the breath of His mouth" (Psalm 33:6). God's word was the agent of creation.

This doctrine is more emphatically stated in the New Testament. *The Gospel of John teaches that Christ at the very beginning of time was there as the Word and He was the divine agent through whom the world was created:* "All things were made through Him, and without Him nothing was made that was made" (1:3). Paul also understood that Christ was the Father's agent in Creation. He spoke of "one Lord Jesus Christ, through whom are all things" (1 Corinthians 8:6). He spoke of "God who created all things through Jesus Christ" (Ephesians 3:9). Again, he said, "For by Him all things were created that are in heaven and that are on earth, visible and invisible, whether thrones or dominions or principalities or powers. All things were created through Him and for Him" (Colossians 1:16). The Son is the Father's agent, the instrument in Creation. This is the meaning of the phrase "through Him." Not only is Christ the mediator of salvation but of all creation.

The agency of the Son in Creation does not deny that the Father is the maker of heaven and earth. The Father functioned as the fountainhead of Creation. He is the source of all things. Though the Son was truly involved in Creation, His role was not that of fountainhead. He was the agent of Creation through whom God brought into existence the world. This truth indicates that Christ, the eternal Word, stands in a special relationship with the world and gives us reason for rejoicing. Yet a greater reason to rejoice is that "the Word became flesh" (John 1:14) and is the Redeemer who will deliver creation from the disastrous consequences of Adam's sin (Romans 8:18-22). So the Son is more than the agent through whom everything came into existence; He is also the redeemer of creation. For it is God's plan "by Him to reconcile all things to Himself, by Him, whether things on earth or things in heaven, having made peace through the blood of His cross" (Colossians 1:20).

C. Work of the Holy Spirit in Creation

As has been noted, the opening verse of Genesis 1 teaches that God created the material world out of nothing. Only after the Father brought the world into being through the Son do we read about the activity of the Spirit. In Genesis 1:2 the earth lay in a formless condition and in darkness. Like a mother bird hovers over chicks in her nest, the Spirit of God hovered over the face of the waters, bringing order and life out of unformed matter and dispelling the darkness. As the One who organized the material world and energized it with life, the Holy Spirit participated with the Father and the Son in Creation. *The Holy Spirit brought order to the materials that had already been created and made them into one system.* All the beauty in the universe and the laws of nature remind us of the work of the Holy Spirit. The Hebrew word for Spirit (*ruach*) literally means breath or wind. Breathing represents life. As long as we breathe, we are alive. The entire universe was energized by the divine breath, the Spirit of God. The power and energy throughout the universe must be traced to the work of the divine Spirit.

A couple of specific observations can be made about the Spirit's role in Creation. The first is that the Spirit beautified the heavens. For instance, Job 26:13 says, "By His Spirit He adorned the heavens." Evidently a peculiar function of the Holy Spirit was to give beauty and glory to the sun, moon, and stars. So the Spirit decorated the heavens and gave order to the heavenly bodies.

The second observation is that the Spirit gave life in Creation. No doubt the Holy Spirit had an active part in the creation of Adam and Eve. After God formed Adam from the dust of the ground, He "breathed into his nostrils the breath of life" (Genesis 2:7). In this instance it seems the Breath of God and the Spirit of God were the same. The biblical account of the creation of Adam must have prompted the words of Job 33:4: "The Spirit of God has made me, and the breath of the Almighty gives me life." The creative work of the Spirit is to give life. Most likely He gives life to all creation, and particularly human life that is distinctly in the image of God.

To summarize the discussion of the triune God and Creation, we may say that the Father, the Son, and the Holy Spirit worked in perfect harmony to create the world. In light of this fact, nature is not its own creator nor is man the maker of all things. For through Christ, the eternal Word, the Father made the world. Then the Spirit brought order, life, and beauty to creation. So the one true God in three persons brought into being all creation. This was done for God's glory and for our benefit.

The Goodness of God's Creation

God himself proclaims the goodness of creation seven times in the opening chapter of Genesis (vv. 4, 10, 12, 18, 21, 25, 31). Creation is good because God made it good. It was not evil when it came from the hands of the living Creator. After He finished His creative work, God declared that everything He had made was "very good" (v. 31). Everything was created to serve a good purpose. This suggests two facts about the Creation: (1) perfect harmony and order and (2) the basic goodness of all things.

A. Perfect Harmony and Order

God is a God of order. Creation is vast, yet in all of its greatness order prevails. The Creation account gives no hint of disorder. On the contrary, each thing created and every creature had its significance and function in relation to the rest of creation. Animals and plants were given their place and purpose. Adam and Eve were given a unique place in creation. They were created in God's image with the capacity to have a relationship with the Creator. Under God they were set over the world and, like other creatures, blessed with the ability to reproduce their own kind.

The biblical view is that all creation is a system of interdependence. Grass grows in soil. Animals depend on grass. Birds live in the air and fish in water. In its original condition the creation was free of conflict. All things were perfectly adjusted. All living creatures and things were in harmony with the Creator and depended upon Him. Self-sufficiency and rebellion not only led to humankind's loss of fellowship with God, but it also disrupted the harmony and order in creation. The deadly effects of sin may be seen in deserts and wilderness, violence among animals, and in upheavals such as storms and earthquakes. *All creation has been deeply wounded by man's sin and subjected to the misery of conflict, disturbances, and death.* Because of the disruption of unity in nature and the oppressive effects of sin, the whole creation groans and travails in pain. Every part of creation groans in hope of the miracle of the resurrection of God's children (Romans 8:18-23). Only then will creation itself be delivered from its

154

present turmoil and bondage into the liberty of the redeemed children of God.

B. Basic Goodness of All Things

The Genesis account of Creation makes it very clear that everything God created was good. Whether it was matter, plants, animals, light, dry land, heavenly bodies, or the first human pair—they were all pronounced good. Not one of them was less good than any of the others. They all were fitted perfectly to fulfill their place in creation. The good and wise Creator made a good world. Though the curse of sin disrupted the created order, creation still is fundamentally good.

The essential goodness of everything God made has decisive practical significance: all of creation has a good use. But from time to time some people have denied the biblical view of creation. The apostle Paul condemned the doctrinal error that rejected the basic goodness of all creation. An example is his words in 1 Timothy 4:1-5:

> Now the Spirit expressly says that in latter times some will depart from the faith, giving heed to deceiving spirits and doctrines of demons, speaking lies in hypocrisy, having their own conscience seared with a hot iron, forbidding to marry, and commanding to abstain from foods which God created to be received with thanksgiving by those who believe and know the truth. For every creature of God is good, and nothing is to be refused if it is received with thanksgiving; for it is sanctified by the word of God and prayer.

The teaching that creation is evil is inspired by demonic activity that leads people to forsake the truth. Those who disseminate such falsehoods speak "lies in hypocrisy, having their own conscience seared." Paul mentioned two particular teachings that issue from demons. The first is the rejection of the institution of marriage, and the second is the insistence on abstaining from meat and other foods. Both errors grow out of a warped view of creation. Marriage is not necessary to holy living, but to forbid marriage is to deny God's good creation of male and female and to treat sex as evil. Abstaining from certain foods for the sake of health is one matter, but it is quite another to abstain because some foods are thought to be evil. The latter rejects good things that the good God has created. Sex and food can be misused, but all that comes from the good God has some good purpose.

The curse of sin has disrupted the created order, but it still serves our well-being, especially as long as we use it as God intended. The biblical doctrine of Creation should make us thankful and free to enjoy the blessings and benefits of the Creation. Gratitude for God's gifts in creation does not lead to the vanity of asceticism and senseless rejection of material things but to the reception of God's blessings in creation and to responsible living in the world.

Chapter 11

THE SIX DAYS OF CREATION

Biblical history begins with a simple, yet a profound statement. "In the beginning God created the heavens and the earth." There was only God before the creation of the world. The creation is not eternal, for it had a definite beginning. Likewise time had a beginning. Before time there was only God. It seems that as the world began so did time. At the very beginning the heavens and earth were created. But in six days God brought forth life and gave distinct order and form to His creation.

The creation itself is a profound mystery. Pentecostal believers recognize that Genesis 1 has been variously interpreted as a mythological or allegorical account of Creation. But for them the biblical account is historically sound. Convinced that creation cannot be truly understood apart from the biblical account, Pentecostals accept Genesis 1 as the truth regarding the origin of the universe. Consider the details of the Creation narrative.

The Six Days of Creation

After the creation of the heavens and the earth, that is, the universe, God by the word of His power proceeded to finish His work of creation. This completion of His creative work occurred within the framework of six days.

A. The First Day (Genesis 1:3-5)

God called into existence light and divided the light from darkness. In the list of specific creative acts, light had a primary significance. What the source of the light was we are not told, but not until the fourth day did the sun, moon, and stars provide light. Most likely the light of the first day was cosmic light, which had as its source not the heavenly bodies but the Son of God. Thousands of years later John declared, "God is light" (1 John 1:5) and spoke of the Son of God as "the light of the world" (John 8:12). As the Holy Spirit hovered over the dark waters, the Son of God sent forth light that drove back the darkness.

On the first day of Creation there was light that God called "Day." The darkness He called "Night." At the beginning the world did not need the light of the sun any more than it will in the new creation. The light of the new creation will not be the light of the sun or moon "for the glory of God illuminated it. The Lamb is its light" (Revelation 21:23). In the beginning there was no need for the light of the sun. All creation was illuminated by cosmic light that radiated from the Son of God. At the end, the source of light will be the same.

B. The Second Day (Genesis 1:6-8)

God separated the waters above from the waters below and made the firmament, what we call the atmosphere or sky. The atmosphere or expanse between the waters above and below God called "heaven" (v. 8). Isaiah 40:22 says God "stretches out the heavens like a curtain, and spreads them out like a tent to dwell in." The heavens stretched out are the firmament. The Bible describes the magnificence of the heavens as transparent and bright like crystal or sapphire (Exodus 24:10; Ezekiel 1:22). As more is learned about the planets, it becomes increasingly clear how marvelous is the handiwork of God.

C. The Third Day (Genesis 1:9-13)

On this day the waters were gathered together into various places, and dry land and plant life appeared. As the waters receded, a large part of the earth was left dry. The other parts formed oceans, seas, lakes and rivers. The appearance of land made plant life possible. The earth began to produce grass, herbs, and fruit. So by His grace God built into creation the processes of reproduction and growth.

D. The Fourth Day (Genesis 1:14-19)

God called forth light on the first day. That light was not provided by sun, moon, and stars but by the eternal Word, "the true Light which gives light to every man coming into the world" (John 1:9). Not until the fourth day did the heavenly bodies begin to serve as sources of light for the earth. The Bible implies a difference between "the light" (v. 4) and "lights in the firmament" (v. 14). "The light" was absolutely sufficient for the sprouting and flourishing of vegetation before sunlight and moonlight. God appointed "the lights in the firmament" (sun and moon) to provide light for the earth and to regulate by their movements the divisions of time and seasons. The lights in the firmament prepared the way for the creation of animals and human beings.

E. The Fifth Day (Genesis 1:20-23)

The verb *create (bara)* appears in Genesis 1:1 and indicates unprecedented, unique activity of God. The word is used also in verse 21 with reference to sea animals and creatures of the air. Just as God's creation of the universe was unique and distinct, so was the creation of animal life. Fish and fowl became abundant, for God said, "Let the waters abound with an abundance of living creatures, and let birds fly above the earth" (v. 20). Due to God's blessings they were given the capacity to reproduce, and they rapidly multiplied and increased.

F. The Sixth Day (Genesis 1:24-31)

On the third day God called forth dry land and vegetation. But it was not until the sixth day that He created land animals and humans. Scripture classifies the land animals in three groups: cattle (domestic animals), creeping things (small animals), and beasts of the earth (wild animals). Vegetable life appeared before animal life and animal life before human life.

God created man (humans) both male and female. Man was the crowning achievement of God's creative work. Such a statement is not prompted by human pride but by three facts: (1) In the Genesis account more space is devoted to the creation of Adam and Eve than to the rest of the Creation. (2) God gave man and woman dominion over the earth and all its creatures. (3) Unlike other creatures of the earth, Adam and Eve were made in the image of God. The Hebrew word for *image* basically means "something cut out" and suggests the idea of resemblance. It may refer to an idol (Numbers 33:52) or a painting (Ezekiel 23:14). The phrase "image of God" stresses that not only Adam but all human beings have a likeness to God and are God's representatives in the world.

Our resemblance to God does not mean that we are in any sense divine. But it does mean we have been placed over the lower creation, and we are able to some extent to control our environment. Above all, we are created with responsibility to the Creator and with capacity for communion with Him. God does not require of other creatures responsible stewardship nor has He given them the capacity to know the difference between right and wrong. Only human beings are capable of choosing between good and evil and of having fellowship with God and with other human beings. Our moral and spiritual nature distinguishes us from the rest of God's creation.

Our unique place in creation is clearly set forth in these words: "Let Us make man in Our image, according to Our likeness; let them have dominion over the fish of the sea, over the birds of the air, and over the cattle, over all the earth and over every creeping thing that creeps on the earth" (Genesis 1:26). Our spiritual nature and authority over other creatures distinguishes us from the rest of creation. Yet we too are creatures of God who have been placed a little lower than the angels and granted authority over everything God made (see Psalm 8:4-8).

The whole creation and the creation of man was a miracle. God the Holy Spirit breathed life into him "and man became a living being" (Genesis 2:7). But when we compare the creation of humans with the miracle of the creation of the heavens and the earth, humans seem insignificant. The universe is so vast, and in comparison we are so small. God has made us less than divine, but He placed us as the capstone of His work.

Length of the Six Days of Creation

The Genesis account gives no hint of when God created the heavens and the earth out of nothing. After the creation of the whole visible and invisible universe, God brought order and life to creation over a six-day period. The most obvious meaning of the six creative days is that they corresponded to our 24-hour day, but Bible scholars do not agree on the length of the days. Some scholars think the days of creation were long, indefinite periods of time. Others suggest that God revealed the story of Creation to Moses in a series of revelations spread over six days.

The six days of creation can certainly be understood as 24-hour days. But the term *day (yom)* appears in Genesis 1 and 2 with different meanings. First, it is used for light in contrast to darkness: "God called the light Day, and the darkness He called Night" (1:5). Second, each of the six creative days is defined as "the evening and the morning", that is, light and darkness together (1:5, 8, 13, 19, 23, 31). For the Jews a new day began at sunset. It was with the sunset that the Sabbath or a holy day started. Third, *day* refers to the entire period of Creation, including the six days: "This is the history of the heavens and the earth when they were created, in the *day* that the LORD God made the earth and the heavens" (2:4). The phrase "in the day" does not contradict the six days of Genesis 1, but Genesis 2:4 is a summary of Creation. Here *day* equals the whole time in which the Creation occurred. In Psalm 95 the 40 years Israel spent in the wilderness are treated as one day: "Do not harden your hearts . . . as in the *day* of trial in the wilderness. . . . For forty years I was grieved with that generation" (vv. 8, 10). Another passage of Scripture tells "that with the Lord one day is as a thousand years" (2 Peter 3:8).

From evidence in the Bible we can understand why opinions differ as to whether the six days refer to 24-hour days or to indefinite periods of time. Those who insist the days of Creation refer to normal calendar days appeal to the formula "evening and morning." Those who take the view that the creative days are long periods of time stress that not until the fourth day did the sun, moon, and stars provide light. Consequently the first three days were not sun-divided days, even though Scripture mentions that these days had an evening and morning. Still another view is that the first three days were long periods of time and the last three were ordinary days. However, the Bible does not provide any decisive clue as to the length of the six days of Creation. Yet there can be no doubt that God who created the heavens and earth out of nothing was capable of finishing His creative work in six literal days. Whatever view we take, the Bible's account of the Creation must be allowed to stand as the infallible Word of God.

Significance of the Six Days of Creation

God was the absolute beginning of all things. By separate creative acts on the six days He gave life and order to creation. In the first three days (Genesis 1:3-13) God divided the light from the darkness, the lower waters from the upper waters, and the lower waters from the dry land. In the course of the next three days the clouds diminshed to allow the sun, moon, and stars to shine on the earth, and then God created the creatures of sea and air, land animals, and humankind. Nothing in the biblical account of Creation suggests that life emerged by the process of evolution. God is the source of all life and has so structured the world that it is good, orderly, and reliable. Over the created order God gave humankind dominion. So God created an orderly and good world where we can benefit from the goodness of the Creator.

To speak of the original order in the world and the goodness of the Creator does not deny the present reality of disorder and suffering in the world. There exists in this world famine, drought, storms, earthquakes, and disease. According to Scripture the creation of

Adam and Eve was quickly followed by the entry of evil into their hearts. Through them not only did evil enter into the human race but also into the world that God created "very good." Creation was affected by the dreadful consequences of man's sin. As a result we live in a fallen world where there are natural calamities, pain, and disease. These realities create disorder and suffering for all of God's creatures, reminding us that not only the human race but the whole world suffers under the burden of sin. There is suffering for the just and the unjust in this world that God created good.

The naturalistic explanations that are so often given for catastrophes and human suffering fall far short of understanding the disastrous consequences of evil. Pentecostals do not base their faith on a human understanding of life's experiences but on trust in God and His Word. For Pentecostals faith is not so much an intellectual endeavor as a living relationship with the Creator through the Holy Spirit. Living in fellowship with God is the basis for appreciating the wonder of all God did in Creation over against experiences of adversity and suffering. So Pentecostals do not merely seek for an understanding of God's creative work and the conditions of the world but also allow the mystery and greatness of the Creation to fill their hearts. They recognize that the human mind is small and needs to be taught by God's Word and Spirit.

In conclusion, God gave form, order, and life in six days to what He created. He set mankind in an ordered world, for "He has made everything beautiful in its time" (Ecclesiastes 3:11). In spite of the disrupting presence of evil generally, divine order still prevails in the world. A contemplation of the greatness and beauty of God's creative work prompted the psalmist to praise the Creator: "Bless the LORD, O my soul! . . . Who stretch out the heavens like a curtain. . . . You who laid the foundations of the earth, so that it should not be moved forever, You covered it with the deep as with a garment; the waters stood above the mountains. . . . O LORD, how manifold are Your works! In wisdom You have made them all" (Psalm 104:1, 2, 5, 6, 24). The appropriate approach to the doctrine of Creation is that of trust, praise, and worship of the Creator.

Chapter 12

GOD'S CARE
AND
RULE
OF
CREATION

Following the six days of Creation, God "rested on the seventh day from all His work which He had done" (Genesis 2:2). That God rested does not mean He lay down and went to sleep, leaving the creation to take care of itself and exercising no control over it. The verb *rest* (*sabat*) means "to cease." On the seventh day God ceased from His creative work and took pleasure in the goodness of all He had created. This day of rest was unlike the other six days. It had no boundaries of evening and morning. God's pleasure with the world He created has no end. But now His work is that of preservation rather than creation. God continues to sustain and control the universe. Should He withdraw from it even momentarily, it would collapse into nothing (see Colossians 1:17). God's care for and control of the universe has traditionally been referred to as His providence, literally meaning that He looks ahead and plans in advance. So the Creator is the God who rules, sustains, and provides for creation.

God's provision is seen in the order of the universe, the natural processes of life, and the unfolding of history. At the time of their creation, God gave each of His creatures the power to reproduce. The Israelites understood their history to be the outworking of God's call of Abraham. On Mount Moriah, Abraham found God to be One who provides, for there God provided a ram for a burnt offering in the place of Isaac (Genesis 22:13). Abraham called that place "The-Lord-Will-Provide." The divine provision of the ram has assured Pentecostals and other Christians of God's constant care and providence.

For Pentecostals, God is not like an absentee landlord, but One who is personally concerned about His creation. Just as in biblical times, Pentecostals expect God's presence and providence to be manifested not only in the general care of creation but also in extraordinary guidance and works of the Holy Spirit. So Pentecostals see a direct connection between the providential presence of God in Bible times and in the 20th century. God works now in the same ways He did in the days of the patriarchs and apostles.

The providence of God will be considered under three headings: the natural world, history, and suffering.

Providence and the Natural World

Through God's Word, the eternal Christ, the world was made (John 1:13); God upholds "all things by the word of His power (Hebrews 1:3); and in Christ all things are held together (Colossians 1:17). God has given the natural world organization and laws. As a result, there is order and constancy in creation. In large measure, we live in a reliable world, where the seasons occur regularly, where there are continuous revolutions of the earth around the sun, and where animal and plant life remain constant. Order and regularity are characteristic of God's creation.

The psalmist declared, "O LORD, how manifold are Your works! In wisdom You have made them all" (Psalm 104:24). The world has order because the Creator preserves all He has made. Deeply conscious of this, the Levites praised God, saying, "You alone are the LORD; You have made heaven, the heaven of heavens, with all their host, the earth and all things on it, the seas and all that is in them, and You preserve them all" (Nehemiah 9:6). Because of God's constantly sustaining power, the general character and course of the natural world are predictable. The world is not shut off from the Creator. At every moment God upholds the world; therefore, He remains with and directs the creation so that it serves His purpose. God's providential care reminds us of His faithful and wise preservation of Creation.

A. God's Faithfulness in Maintaining Natural Order

The constancy and the reliability of the natural world tells us something about the faithfulness of the living God. The order and stability of the world is something we have come to expect. The regularity of natural things is completely dependent on God's presence and steadfast faithfulness. God promised after the Flood, "While the earth remains, seedtime and harvest, and cold and heat, and winter and summer, and day and night shall not cease" (Genesis 8:22). Jeremiah spoke God's covenant with day and night, saying for the LORD, "If I have not appointed the ordinances [fixed order] of heaven and earth, then I will cast away the descendants of Jacob and David My servant" (33:25, 26).

God has set the limits of everything. The order that prevails in the world points to the goodness and faithfulness of God (see Acts 17:22-30; Romans 1:18-23). As Paul said, "He [God] did not leave Himself without witness, in that He did good, gave us rain from heaven and fruitful seasons" (Acts 14:17). God has so ordered the world and life that we can have confidence in going about our daily activities and making plans for the future. We live in a dependable world—a world where the Creator is faithful to maintain order so that life can be meaningful and lived in an orderly manner. The natural eye may have appreciation for the order of the world and even vaguely comprehend divine providence, but a proper understanding of providence must be rooted in divine revelation, recorded in the Scripture and confirmed by the experience of faith.

B. God's Faithfulness in the Preservation of Creatures

As taught in Scripture, God's providential care is not subject to fortune and fate. A sparrow does not fall "to the ground apart from your father's will" (Matthew 10:29). Certainly, if God directs the flight of birds, then we must be constrained to confess with the psalmist that "the LORD our God, who dwells on high ... humbles Himself to behold the things that are in the heavens and in the earth" (Psalm 113:5, 6). Marvelous is God's faithfulness in preserving and sustaining each of His creatures, especially men and women. God provides for the fish and the birds and sustains all things in their own uniqueness. The Bible assures us that God preserves "man and beast" (Psalm 36:6). Yet Jesus said we are "of more value than many sparrows" (Matthew 10:31). All life is constantly and vigorously preserved by the power of God.

At this point let us reflect on the marvel of our own physical existence. The heart begins to beat before birth and continues until death. Blood circulates through the body and carries red and white cells that are vital to life. The red blood cells are carried to the lungs, where they take up oxygen. All of this goes on from moment to moment, yet without any effort on our part. Indeed, it is remarkable that we stay alive. There can be but one ultimate source: the living God, who gives us breath and enables our hearts to keep up their life beat. Life itself testifies of God's faithfulness. Never should we cease to praise Him for the gift of life.

Our God is not an idle God. He continuously involves Himself in the preservation of His creatures by providing for their needs. The unfailing goodness of God is expressed beautifully in the words of the psalmist: "And You give them their food in due season. You open Your hand and satisfy the desire of every living thing" (Psalm 145:15, 16). God's concern extends to all people, for Jesus declared that God "makes His sun rise on the evil and on the good, and sends rain on the just and on the unjust" (Matthew 5:45). With the assurance of God's unfailing provisions we may live free of anxiety, especially if we know Him as our heavenly Father. As Jesus said, the Father knows what our needs are. Since He cares for the birds of the air and the lilies of the field, surely we should not be overwhelmed with worry about the necessities of life (see Matthew 6:25-34).

Jesus said, "Seek first the kingdom of God and His righteousness, and all these things [necessities] shall be added to you" (v. 33). We can be assured that God, who has given to us the greatest gift, His own Son, will not withhold lesser blessings. God has richly provided for our spiritual needs in Christ, but He will "also freely give us all things" (Romans 8:32). This promise does not mean that we may not experience dangers and perils (8:35-39), but the foundation for our victory was laid at Calvary. God is the protector and history maker of those who trust in Him. Though Paul experienced many adversities, he was convinced that divine preservation protects from evil those who belong to Christ. To emphasize this truth, he wrote these words:

"But the Lord is faithful, who will establish you and guard you from the evil one" (2 Thessalonians 3:3). Many believers know by experience that God does protect His people—from evil and the Evil One.

C. God's Faithfulness to Renew Creation

The continuous work of God is demonstrated by His constant renewal of the creation. Scripture makes direct reference to this aspect of divine providence and draws particular attention to the renewal of the creation by the Holy Spirit. The work of the Holy Spirit is not restricted to the Christian experience of the new birth, sanctification, and empowerment for service. The ministry of the Spirit encompasses more than that. At the very beginning the Holy Spirit brought order and life to the creation, and the Spirit continues to exercise providential care over it. In Psalm 104:30 we find reference to God's preservation and renewal of the creation: "You send forth Your Spirit, they are created; and You renew the face of the earth." The psalmist affirmed the creative work of the Spirit in general; but He also spoke of renewal, which is constantly evident in the world, especially in the season of spring. Isaiah recognized the Holy Spirit's power to renew and transform the material world: "Until the Spirit is poured upon us from on high, and the wilderness becomes a fruitful field, and the fruitful field is counted as a forest" (32:15). Doubtlessly this passage refers to spiritual revival and the outpouring of the Spirit at Pentecost.

Nevertheless, it reminds us that luxuriant growth in the plant world is also the result of the work of the Holy Spirit.

The Holy Spirit is vital to the preservation and renewal of the natural realm. The outpouring of the Spirit brings power and revival in the spiritual realm. Likewise the sustaining and renewal of the natural realm are intimately related to the Holy Spirit. The beauty of creation, plants beside flowing streams, flowers in the autumn, the daily horizon of the sky—all these delights are a testimony to the sustaining providence of the Creator and the continual work of the Holy Spirit in the natural world.

Providence and History

The living God is Lord of the entire course of history. Because of God's rule there is order in history as well as nature. From the beginning God has been directing history to accomplish His purpose. But He has controlled history while giving us freedom of choice. He wills that we be free, with the capacity to chose between good and evil. In spite of God's providential goodness, Adam and Eve misused their freedom by disobeying God. Since then, sin and rebellion have increased in the world. Nevertheless God has not ceased to be the Lord of all.

As the narrative of the Bible unfolds, it becomes clear that history proceeded according to God's plan and His prophets were able to foretell events that would happen. The history of Israel was in the hands of God. The nation of Israel began with God's call of Abraham. Their enslavement in Egypt ended with the miracle of deliverance and a subsequent covenant at Mount Sinai. After a generation in the wilderness, they settled in Canaan. They lived in that land under the rule of the judges and then under the kings. Following that they were exiled in Assyria and Babylon, and eventually groups of exiles returned to their homeland. God's providential guidance of Israel's history revealed His grace and judgments.

The focus of the Old Testament is on the nation of Israel. But the fortunes of other nations were also in the hands of God. Exodus 9:13-

17 tells of God's dealing with Egypt when Pharaoh refused to set Israel free from bondage. Daniel 8 and 11 foretold the four kingdoms into which the empire of Alexander the Great would be divided. Scripture clearly reveals that history proceeds as divinely planned. God directs the affairs of the world because He controls history. Individuals have misused and still do misuse their freedom, but in spite of human wrongdoing, God overrules and fulfills His eternal plan for the world (see Genesis 50:20).

God has shown Himself to be personally concerned with the life and history of the human race. Fully convinced of this fact, Paul said that God "has made from one blood every nation of men to dwell on all the face of the earth, and has determined their preappointed times and the boundaries of their habitation" (Acts 17:26). It is not due to chance that nations have arisen and people have spread over the face of the earth. God has given humans the earth for a home and has appointed the location for each nation to dwell. The purpose of God's care of people and nations is "so that they should seek the Lord . . . and find Him" (v. 27). It is His desire that all people come to know Him.

It must be emphasized that God is concerned for all people. According to Scripture, Israel occupies a special place in God's purpose of salvation for the world, but God's choice of Israel did not exclude other nations from His purpose. God asked through the prophet Amos, "Did I not bring up Israel from the land of Egypt, the Philistines from Caphtor, and the Syrians from Kir?" (9:7). The Old Testament teaches that the direction of Israel's history was a strong concern of God. But He is Lord of all history— the Lord of the Philistines, the Syrians, and all other nations. He also cares for them and directs their destiny.

The Bible declares that God providentially guides people and nations. In no way does divine providence deny freedom to act and power to choose good or evil. Never has the convergence of human freedom and divine providence been more graphically demonstrated than in the death of Jesus Christ. The powerful words of Peter at Pentecost laid the responsibility for Jesus' death directly on the Jews, but it happened according to the plan of God. Jesus Christ "being delivered by the determined counsel and foreknowledge of God, you have taken by lawless hands, have crucified, and put to death" (Acts 2:23), Peter said. Lawless men did evil in putting Christ to death, but God did not do evil, nor did He will it. Men like Herod and Pilate, as well as the Jews, became guilty of the cruel death of Jesus. Yet, they also freely fulfilled the plan of God. Through His mighty power God made the cross the means by which He saves us.

The crucifixion of the Lord Jesus confronts us with the mystery of the divine plan being fulfilled in and through human events. At the Cross it was as though God momentarily pulled back the curtain before our eyes to give us a glimpse into the profound mystery of His rule in history. The Christ of Calvary was "the Lamb slain from the foundation of the world" (Revelation 13:8). In IIis death the Redeemcr embodied the faithfulness and providence of the Creator.

In the New Testament the providence of God has great significance for the Christian life. God's eternal purpose was to send Christ and to save us through Him (see Ephesians 3:11). The success of His saving work was foreordained of God and sure. At the same time, God appeals to us by His Word and Spirit to accept His gracious work of redemption in Christ. The appropriation of salvation requires a response on our part—a response of faith. The divine side and the human side of salvation must be kept in proper focus. Speaking of the divine side, Paul wrote, "It is God who works in you both to will and to do for His good pleasure" (Philippians 2:13). But from the human side he said, "Work out your own salvation with fear and trembling" (v. 12).

These words plainly say that salvation is of God, but it also calls for our constant effort in pursuing the Christian life.

Divine providence does not take away our freedom. For those who trust in His grace, God's rule in the world is their source of hope and comfort in all of life's experiences. Paul summarized the Christian view of divine providence in this statement: "We know that all things work together for good to those who love God, to those who are the called according to His purpose" (Romans 8:28). The continuing presence of God with us in Christ is assurance that all things are made to serve good. Christ came to the earth and entered the depths of human suffering. When He returned to heaven, He did not forsake His people. As He told the disciples, "I am with you always, even to the end of the age" (Matthew 28:20). So He sent the Holy Spirit to be the continuing presence of God with us. We live on the A.D. side of Pentecost, where God is with us through the powerful presence of His Spirit, even to the end of the world.

As history moves toward the second coming of Christ, God continues to work all things together for good. Amid the presence of evil, the attacks of Satan, and the suffering in the world, God remains in control. But God's rule in the world is a mystery which can be penetrated only by relying on the Scriptures and the Holy Spirit to give insight into the divine purpose. The certainty of the fulfillment of God's plan in history was stated emphatically by Paul:

> Oh, the depth of the riches both of the wisdom and knowledge of God! How unsearchable are His judgments and His ways past finding out! . . . For of Him and through Him and to Him are all things, to whom be glory forever. Amen *(Romans 11:33, 36).*

How unlimited are the resources of God's wisdom and

power! Throughout the history of the world, from the Creation to the final consummation, God rules in history and will finally bring His creation to its goal.

Providence and Suffering

Pentecostal Christians affirm that God is good, but like everybody else they live in a suffering world. The Bible acknowledges the reality of suffering and evil. Some people have sought to deal with these problems by unbridled optimism, as if there were no tribulations, pain, and evil. Divine providence does not mean that because God provides there will be only happiness and serenity on earth. Pretending that evil does not exists does not remove the difficulties created by its presence. The practice of the power of positive thinking does not turn evil into good. Refusing to acknowledge evil and suffering does nothing to improve life.

The biblical doctrine of providence is profoundly realistic. In no way does providence deny the suffering of the righteous (Psalm 34:19). The Good Shepherd allows His sheep to go through dark valleys and sore afflictions (Psalm 23:4). Christians look forward to the new earth and heaven, but Scripture recognizes that trials and tribulations are the plight of the world until the end of the age. Before the final battle between God and the powers of evil, there will be wars and rumors of wars, nation against nation, famines, pestilences, earthquakes, sorrows, tribulations, and false prophets (see Matthew 24:4-14).

Uncompromising realism about suffering is set forth in the same Bible that says God is good and all of His creatures are under His providential care and guardianship. Pain or suffering can be more easily endured if there is reasonable explanation for it. For example, we know it is normal to feel pain in doing strenuous exercise and to suffer from aching muscles as a result. God has made us with the capacity to feel pain. Some suffering is inevitable. But too much suffering, pain, and misery seem to have no useful purpose. How can we insist that God is compassionate and all-powerful when the world is so full of misery? Pentecostals recognize that the suffering of the righteous, as told in the Book of Job, provokes questions. Yet Pentecostals affirm the biblical view of divine providence and take seriously the troubles of the world such as wars, injustice, deformed children, natural catastrophes, extreme poverty, starvation and death. Given the extent of the reality of pain and evil in our world, we must realize that easy answers are not adequate and some aspects of suffering must remain in the sphere of hidden things that belong to God (see Deuteronomy 29:29).

A. The Fact of Suffering

Never is the Bible casual or naive about suffering and evil. It speaks of the suffering of both people and the whole physical creation (Genesis 3:14-19; Romans 8:19-22). Should we conclude that God is too weak to do anything about evil and suffering? Or is He unjust and the cause of the world's troubles? To respond to these kinds of questions, let us consider what Scripture teaches about suffering and evil.

1. God's Capacity for Suffering

It must not be thought that God does not feel pain and grief. In spite of the wonders wrought in Egypt, Israel disobeyed God in the wilderness and grieved His heart (Psalm 78:40; Hebrews 3:10, 17). By their rebellion the people of Israel also grieved the Holy Spirit (Isaiah 63:10; cf. Ephesians 4:30). When Jesus met the man with a withered hand, He was grieved

178

by the Pharisees' hardness of heart (Mark 3:5). Jesus demonstrated again and again that He was "a Man of sorrows and acquainted with grief" (Isaiah 53:3). He wept at the tomb of Lazarus (John 11:35) and over the city of Jerusalem (Luke 19:41). In the agony of Gethsemane He "offered up prayers and supplications, with vehement cries and tears" (Hebrews 5:7). He experienced all sorts of testings and rejections. He endured the cruel insults and buffetings in His trial before Caiaphas, Pilate, and Herod. And, finally, He died a most shameful and painful death as He hung on a wooden cross. The Bible clearly teaches that suffering not only belongs to human experience but is also known to the triune God. Father, Son, and Holy Spirit also feel pain and suffering. For God to love as He does means that He suffers much. The suffering of the Cross was the supreme manifestation and measure of divine love. The amazing love of God poured out in our hearts by the Holy Spirit more than compensates for any afflictions or pain (Romans 5:5).

2. Causes of Suffering

The reality of suffering is the awful result of the sin in the world and human life. The world created by God was "very good." So suffering is not due to the kind of world God made. But when Adam and Eve rebelled, their sin brought great suffering on the human race as well as the whole creation (Genesis 3:14-19; Romans 8:20-22). Universal suffering is the direct result of their disobedience. The entry of sin into the human race has caused pain and interferes with the enjoyment of life. Often people suffer because of their own wrongdoing or that of others. The words of Paul come to mind: "Whatever a man sows, that he will also reap" (Galatians 6:7). Evil deeds and self-indulgence produce disorders affecting body, mind, and spirit. Wrongdoing leads to personal guilt and pangs of remorse, as revealed in

179

Psalms 32 and 51.

Unforgiven sins can have serious consequences for the physical health of an individual. Many mental and emotional problems are due to sin and guilt. Without question, much suffering caused by ignorance might have been avoided. And suffering occurs because of natural calamities, such as storms, earthquakes, and deadly bacteria and diseases. Individuals are subject to aging, which eventually leads to suffering and death. The worldwide dimensions of suffering is evidence of the grim consequences of sin.

B. Purposes of Suffering

Undoubtedly, suffering is a result of God's punishment of sin. Besides that, Scripture indicates that suffering serves two other purposes.

1. Suffering Is God's Way of Warning the Sinner

The judgment of God may bring great suffering and serve as His call to repentance and renewal. When the judgments of God come upon the earth, Isaiah says, "the inhabitants of the world will learn righteousness" (26:9). The outpouring of divine judgment will make for widespread and intense suffering (Revelation 16:8, 9). God sends calamity upon people as a penalty for their sins (Isaiah 45:7). So suffering and calamities may very well be used by God to summon men and women to turn from their sins to God.

We should not assume that suffering always corresponds to the evil a person has done. Some good people have endured great suffering. But some evildoers have appeared to live relatively free of suffering in this life. Jesus spoke about the error of thinking that the degree of one's suffering is always determined by the extent of one's sin. He spoke of 18 people who were killed when a tower in Siloam fell on them and asked, "Do you think that they were worse sinners than all other men who dwelt in Jerusalem?" (Luke 13:4). Obviously the 18 were not innocent, but many were more sinful than those on whom the tower fell. But it seems they perished without repentance, for this tragedy prompted Jesus to say, "Unless you repent you will all likewise perish" (v. 5). The sudden death of the 18 served as a warning to repent before it is too late.

2. Suffering Is a Means of Discipline

The walk of faith is inevitably accompanied by suffering. Those whom God loves He chastens and disciplines (Hebrews 12:5-11). Though painful, it is spiritually profitable for the child of God. As Christians we may view suffering in these ways:

a. *Suffering develops character and deepens commitment to Christ.* Paul, who had suffered much for his faith, wrote, "Tribulation produces perseverance; and perseverance, character; and character, hope" (Romans 5:3, 4). Strong Christian character is produced by learning to endure adversities with faith and fortitude. When we suffer for Christ, the sure outcome of holding on to faith is growth in character and deepening of obedience to God. Our supreme example is the Lord Jesus, who demonstrated that the way of obedience is the way of suffering. "He learned obedience by the things which He suffered" (Hebrews 5:8). It is not that Jesus suffered for disobedience. He was sinless, but He learned by the experience of suffering what obedience to God involves. At times the cost is great in doing the will of God and may call for us to endure the buffetings of Satan, physical hardships, and mental anguish. Doubtlessly, suffering is used by God to develop our faith, humility, and patience—in short, to produce strong character.

b. *Suffering is sharing the sufferings of Christ.* The desire of Paul was to know Christ in the fellowship of His sufferings, being conformed constantly to His death (Philippians 3:10). Sharing in the sufferings of Christ has eternal value for the believer (1 Peter 1:11; Romans 8:17, 18). But as Paul indicated, its significance does not lie only in our future inheritance of eternal life. Close fellowship with Christ's sufferings deepens our knowledge of the Savior. Where believers share in the sufferings of the Lord, their relationship with Him becomes deeper and deeper. This kind of relationship was in view when Paul said he counted "all things loss for the excellence of the knowledge of Christ Jesus my Lord" (Philippians 3:8). Our fellowship with the Lord was made possible by His sufferings and is maintained and deepened as we share in His sufferings. All who suffer for the sake of Christ can have a deeper knowledge of Christ and a more profound sense of His presence.

c. *Suffering is a cause for rejoicing.* No one can read far in the New Testament without coming across a striking concept, namely, that sharing in Christ's sufferings is a blessing that gives believers reason for joy. Jesus pronounced a blessing on those who suffer persecution for the sake of righteousness (Matthew 5:10). After the apostles had been beaten for preaching the gospel, they were released and sent away, "rejoicing that they were counted worthy to suffer shame" for the name of Jesus (Acts 5:41). One of those apostles was Peter. Knowing personally what it meant to suffer for the gospel, he later wrote to Christians undergoing a "fiery trial." He said to them, "Rejoice to the extent that you partake of Christ's sufferings, that when His glory is revealed, you may also be glad with exceeding joy"

(1 Peter 4:13).

d. *Those who walk the way of faith and holiness are certain to experience suffering.* Such a walk inevitably places them in opposition to the world and Satan. But "count it all joy when you fall into various trials" (James 1:2). Suffering for the sake of the gospel is preparation for coming glory. The Holy Spirit assures believers that present suffering is momentary and "light affliction" when compared to the "eternal weight of glory" (2 Corinthians 4:17). Eternal glory will far outweigh the trials and tribulations we endure in this life.

C. Mystery of Suffering

Though the causes and purposes of suffering have been noted, we will not fully understand divine providence until we see Christ face-to-face (see 1 Corinthians 13:12). It remains a mystery why some Christians are chosen to suffer more than others. Believers do not know the future nor what is best for them, but God knows both. So at times we cannot see what God is trying to accomplish through the sufferings of His people. His aim may be to correct imperfections that are not readily seen. He may be preparing us to accomplish a specific task that will in some way serve His own glory. Suffering has prepared many Christians to minister comfort and hope to others.

From our limited point of view, so much pain and suffering seem to be needless and meaningless. But none of us can penetrate fully the mystery of divine providence. Yet by the aid of the Holy Spirit we can appreciate the goodness of God. Paul's realization of how good God is prompted Him to write these Spirit-inspired words: "How unsearchable are His judgments and His ways past finding out!" (Romans 11:33). That was the response of faith. Strong faith in the living God enables us to live in the midst of sufferings and dangers without bitterness and despair. Job's faith enabled him to exclaim, "Though He slay me, yet will I trust Him" (13:15). There are no completely satisfactory answers to all of our problems. Nevertheless, God's grace is sufficient for our needs; and He is to be trusted, praised, and worshiped.

Part Four:
DOCTRINE
OF
MAN

Chapter 13

HUMANKIND: A SPECIAL CREATION

Only humankind can rightfully be understood as the most special of the creatures God made to live on earth. As a result, Pentecostals root and ground their view of human nature in what the Scriptures say about our origin and relationship with God. So they not only turn to the Bible to answer the question "Who is God?" but also to answer the question "What is man?"

Philosophers, social scientists, and religious thinkers have offered a wide range of various explanations of the nature of human beings. Doubtlessly some of these ideas are true, but their conclusions are based on limited observations. As a result, something fundamental is missing from all their views. The only way we can truly understand the full dimensions of human nature is from a theological perspective. This is the perspective found in the Scriptures, where the true dimensions of human nature are described and humans are seen as a special creation.

The Origin of Adam and Eve

According to the Genesis account, God created humankind male and female (1:27). As the natural world had a beginning, so did Adam and Eve. They were a special creation of God, created in the very image of God. That fact made them similar to God and distinct from the rest of the living creatures. However, this biblical view of the origin of humans has been challenged by modern theories of human evolution.

A. The Evolutionary Explanation

Proponents of evolution propose that humans sprang from animal forms of life. But the evidence is not sufficient to prove that one species of life can evolve from another. If the evolution of humans did occur, then our conclusion would be that human beings did not spring from one ancestor but from a number of ancestors. But according to the Bible, Adam was the first man and the entire human family descended from him.

The genealogical table of 1 Chronicles 1 begins with Adam. Since the other people included in this list were real people, Adam should not be viewed as an exception. Luke traced the ancestry of Jesus back to Adam, and he called Adam "the son of God" (Luke 3:23-38). Adam was the beginner and earthly father of the human race. To see Adam as a result of an evolutionary process would force us to regard the biblical account of Creation as a myth. Instead, the biblical account of the creation of humankind is history and fact. It indicates that Adam was a fresh creation and gives no hint of his emerging from lower forms of life. There is no direct link, as the evolutionists assume, between humans and the animal world. Therefore the so-called missing link will never be found.

B. The Biblical Explanation

Scripture has a totally different perspective on the origin of

Adam and Eve. According to Genesis 1:26, God said, "Let Us make man in Our image, according to Our likeness." The next verse says, "God created man in His own image." That is to say, the image in which Adam and Eve were created made them human, distinguishing them from the rest of God's creatures. Their creation was the result of the direct action of God. Adam came into being by the immediate creation of God, who formed him from the dust of the ground (Genesis 2:7). Eve also was created immediately by God. Nothing in the biblical account points to the evolving of Eve from a lower form of life. A deep sleep came upon Adam. God removed a rib from Adam and fashioned Eve from the rib He took from Adam's body. Like her husband, she was a new being, created by God in His own image. By His almighty power, God brought all things, man and woman included, into existence. "All things were made through Him, and without Him nothing was made that was made" (John 1:3). Only God is capable of creating personal beings.

Creation and Union of Body and Spirit

God created Adam a physical and spiritual being. Some believe in a twofold division of man (dichotomy). This view proposes that the words *soul* and *spirit* are used interchangeably to describe the spiritual nature of man. According to the dichotomous view, man consists of two parts: body and spirit (or soul). So the words *soul* and *spirit* are thought to be different terms for our spiritual nature. A number of scriptures imply that man is essentially physical and spiritual in nature (Romans 8:10; 1 Corinthians 5:5; Ephesians 2:3).

Others teach a threefold division of man's nature (trichotomy). This view proposes that we are made up of three distinct parts: body, soul, and spirit. Ordinarily, trichotomists define the spirit as the highest part of human nature, giving humans the capacity for communion with God. The soul is regarded as the seat of natural human life. For biblical support of trichotomy, appeals are made to the passage in 1 Thessalonians 5:23, where the three words—body, soul, and spirit—are used to describe the whole person (cf. Hebrews 4:12). Whatever view of human nature is embraced, the emphasis of Scripture is on the unity of human nature. That is, each person has a physical and spiritual nature. These two dimensions of human nature are united in each person. The biblical account of Adam's creation teaches clearly that he was a physical and spiritual being. The manner in which he was created bears out this uniqueness.

A. The Human Body

The physical nature of Adam was a distinctive creation of God. The physical body was given to humans by the Creator and is just as much from God as the spiritual side of human nature. God formed man's body from "the dust of the ground" (Genesis 2:7) as He did the animals (2:19). So the physical body of humans has much in common with that of the animals, especially the mammals. The human body was made of earth and shares the same elements as God's other creatures.

Many times the Scriptures affirm that Adam was formed from the earth. Because of his disobedience to God, Adam was required by sweat and pain to eke out a living from the ground, to which he would return in the end (Genesis 3:19). To God, Job said, "Remember, I pray, that You have made me like clay. And will You turn me into dust again?" (10:9). The psalmist spoke of God who "knows our frame; He remembers that we are dust" (Psalm 103:14). The New Testament also teaches that the human body is dust. All humans are made of "dust" (1 Corinthians 15:47, 48).

Other terms are used by the biblical writers to speak of the human body as material element. The term *flesh* illustrates this point. At times *flesh* refers to natural descent. For example, Jesus "was born of the seed of David according to the flesh" (Romans 1:3). Or *flesh* may have reference to the sinful nature, as it does in Romans 8:1, 5-9. But *flesh* may also refer to the human body: "The life which I now live in the flesh I live by faith in the Son of God" (Galatians 2:20). "We have this treasure in earthen vessels" (2 Corinthians 4:7). That is, although Christians have the gospel of Christ, they still live in frail, mortal bodies. So the Scriptures affirm many times that humans are corporal beings and our bodies are from the dust of the earth.

B.   The Breath (Spirit) of Life

Scripture recognizes the distinction between the physical and spiritual nature of man, but God is the author of both. Having made the human body from the dust of the earth, God breathed into it the breath of life and "man became a living being" (Genesis 2:7). When God breathed into man's nostrils the breath of life, it was a special divine act. By this supernatural act, Adam was created in a unique relationship with God. The Spirit of God breathed into him physical life and also endued him with spiritual capacities for fellowship with God. His spiritual nature was derived from God's Spirit. At death, the human spirit leaves the body and returns to God who gave it (Psalm 146:4; Ecclesiastes 12:7). So humans have in them the physical breath of life as do the animals, but humans are also spiritual. The spirit that God breathed into the first man set him apart from all the other creatures and gave him a unique relationship with the Creator.

We need to guard against confusing the human spirit with the Spirit of God. The human spirit is an aspect of human nature but is not identical with the divine Spirit. Humans are not divine. But the human spirit is the means through which God deals with us and reveals Himself to us. "The Spirit Himself bears witness with our spirit that we are children of God" (Romans 8:16). So the Spirit of God, who indwells each believer, speaks to the human spirit and makes believers so keenly aware that they are the children of God that they cry "Abba, Father" (8:15). Moreover, when believers speak in tongues, they utter mysteries by the power of the Holy Spirit (1 Corinthians 14:2). Yet it is through the human spirit, directly influenced by the Holy Spirit, that they speak. As told by Paul, "For if I pray in a tongue, my spirit prays" (14:14). The Scriptures and experience confirm that the human spirit is a vehicle for communion with God. This is seen in the words of Mary's song: "My soul magnifies the Lord, and my spirit has rejoiced in God my Savior" (Luke 1:46, 47).

C. A Living Being

Adam was the result of the Spirit of God breathing life into a body of earth. At that moment the two natures of Adam were united. He was made a living soul by the Holy Spirit. Both sides of his personality—the physical and spiritual—were vital to his being. Therefore, the body of man should not be treated as something low and inferior. The body was created by God and is not to be regarded with contempt. Everything God made was "very good" (Genesis 1:31). The origin of man in his totality was a miraculous event.

The view of Pentecostals is that God is the God of the whole person. Pentecostals take the whole of human nature seriously, recognizing that each person has physical as well as spiritual needs and that the life of faith encompasses all dimensions of human nature. The body is not a mere incident of personal existence nor is it simply a shell for the soul. For it was not until the union of body and spirit that Adam became a living, conscious being. The body is good and necessary for human life. Christ took upon Himself a body. At times the body appears to stand for the whole person. That was the case when Paul spoke about the union of the believer's body with Christ and the Holy Spirit making the human body His temple (1 Corinthians 6:15, 19). "Therefore," he said, "glorify God in your body" (v. 20). As in the present life, the body will be a vital dimension of future life. In the resurrection, believers in Christ will have spiritual bodies (15:44).

The Man-Woman Partnership

Scripture makes it clear that humans were created for social relationships. The social relations between man and woman further indicate that they are a special creation of God. God created animals and man both male and female. So sexual differences did not distinguish the first pair from all the other creatures, but their capacity for love and fellowship with one another did. After God created Adam, He said, "It is not good that man should be alone; I will make him a helper comparable to him" (2:18). God wills that humans live in fellowship and community in love. None of the animals proved to be suitable as a companion for Adam. So God caused a deep sleep to fall on Adam and took from him a rib to form the woman.

Upon being presented with the woman, Adam declared, "This is now bone of my bones and flesh of my flesh; she shall be called Woman (*Ishshah*), because she was taken out of Man (*Ish*)" (Genesis 2:23). The word *woman* is derived from the word for *man*. She was taken from man. More than that, the first human pair were husband and wife, indicating the fact of two sexes. The inseparable union that exists between husband and wife is stressed further by the statement "A man shall leave his father and mother and be joined to his wife, and they shall become one flesh" (2:24). So woman was created to share man's life. Because she is "bone" of his "bones" and "flesh" of his "flesh," man cannot realize his true nature without her.

The very nature of man and woman calls for them to live in community. They are beings who belong to one another and were created to live in community and love. The husband-wife relationship has broad implications for all of human life. Individuals cannot realize their true nature without others. So we come together and work together. Human existence is existence in community and fellowship. Only by living in fellowship with God and with our fellows can we be truly human.

Perhaps we will better understand the Creation account of the man-woman relationship by observing that (1) God himself exists in fellowship and (2) a proper relationship with God is vital to human relations.

God Exists in Community

The Father, Son, and Holy Spirit are joined by the closest ties of love, common purpose, and character. The inner life of the Trinity is characterized by fellowship and communion. God is not alone, for the Father, the Son, and the Holy Spirit live in fellowship. As the Creator lives in fellowship, so He created male and female so that man should not be alone. From the outset God intended humans to live in partnership. As the triune God himself lives in fellowship and mutuality, He wills that His human creatures live in community.

So God's creation of man was not complete until He created a pair of human beings, Adam and Eve. When God provided Eve as Adam's partner, then the creation of man was finished. Just as there is unity in the Godhead (God is God) and there are distinctions (Father, Son, Holy Spirit), we find the same to be true of human beings. Man is man but two distinct sexes: male and female. The first pair were not simply man and woman but husband and wife. The coming together of man and woman in marriage clearly indicated that God made them to complement one another. God willed that they live in fellowship and communion.

"Therefore a man shall leave his father and mother and be joined to his wife, and they shall become one flesh" (Genesis 2:24). As husband and wife Adam and Eve became one, but they remained two distinct persons. The most intimate human relationship reflects God's own being, who is one but exists in three persons.

A proper relationship with God is vital to human relations. By their own choice Adam and Eve rebelled against the divine will and chose to live independently of God. Their relationship with one another should have prepared them for a higher relationship—the love of the Creator and communion with Him. God created them to live in communion with one another and their fellows. But they were also capable of living in communion with God. From the very beginning the full development of their human capacities was not to be the most significant dimension of their existence, but rather their acceptance of God's love by continuing in fellowship with Him.

According to the narrative of Genesis 2, Adam was aware of God's constant love, care, and presence. God put him in the Garden of Eden and gave him the privilege of eating of every tree of the garden except the Tree of Knowledge of Good and Evil. God brought the animals to Adam so he could give names to each one. God spoke to Adam telling him what he should and should not do, making him responsible for his actions. God took Eve from Adam's side and brought her to him. Then after Adam and Eve were deceived by the serpent, God walked in the cool of the day to have fellowship with them (Genesis 3:8). Only through living in communion and fellowship with God could they have had the best human existence.

Adam and Eve were created man and woman, husband and wife. But vital to all their relationships was a third partner, namely God himself. In fact, first and foremost was their relationship with Him. It is important for us to recognize that true community and binding relationships involve three parties: God, self, and fellow human beings. This triune relationship reflects the nature of the triune God. We have been made for fellowship with God and our fellows. But first we stand before God and second beside other human beings. By continuing in fellowship with God we have the basis for building mutual and lasting relationships with others. As we abide in communion with God and with our fellows who stand beside us, we find our true nature and the purpose for which God created us. As the human spirit needs the body, so we need relationship with God as well as with one another. For we were created by God in love and to be persons of love.

Chapter 14

HUMANKIND
IN THE
IMAGE
OF
GOD

As a special creation of God, man (male and female) was created in the image of God. The Bible tells in Genesis 1:27, "So God created man in His own image; in the image of God He created him; male and female He created them." Of all the living creatures, man alone is described as being in the image of God. The image of God made Adam and Eve distinctively human and uniquely different from all other creatures of our world.

It should not be thought that the image of God was only in Adam and Eve. Every human being is created in God's image. The Bible says that Adam "begot a son in his own likeness, after his image, and named him Seth" (Genesis 5:3). So the image and likeness of God was transmitted to Seth through his parents.

Every person bears God's image. For this reason, murder is an attack on the image of God and is forbidden by Scripture (Genesis 9:6). Faithful to biblical teaching, Pentecostal theology places an emphasis on the dignity of every person and the sacredness of human life. The image of God is the most distinctive dimension of human existence. To understand the essence of humanity we need to know what the biblical writers meant when they spoke of the image of God in man.

The Biblical Idea of the Image of God

The Hebrew word (*tselem*) translated *image* has the basic meaning "something cut out" (Genesis 1:26; 5:l; 9:6). An image is an outline or shadow of a figure. It can refer to an idol (Numbers 33:52) or to a painting (Ezekiel 23:14). But the term "image of God" has a special theological significance. As viewed from God's perspective, the image of God in man is explained as "according to Our likeness" (Genesis 1:26). Image and likeness are basically the same. God made us like Himself. As a child comes into existence in the likeness of his father and mother, so we resemble God himself. Created in the likeness of God, man was made to reflect the qualities of God's character. Like God we have the power to think, will, and feel. The image of God in man may be defined as higher powers of conscious life that distinguish man from the other creatures of God.

In His creative wisdom, God made man to resemble Himself. But this resemblance does not mean humans are divine. We are less than the Creator but more than the other creatures in whom the divine image does not appear. Neither the term *image* nor the term *likeness* is found in Psalm 8. The psalmist said that man is less than the angels but God has crowned him with glory and honor (v. 5). These majestic words, *glory* and *honor*, summarize our likeness to God. Ranking just a little below the angels, we are to reflect God's likeness and glory. The majesty of God is best reflected not by the moon and the stars in the heavens but by His creatures made in His image. The image of God affects the entire pattern of human life. It bestows on us our value in God's sight.

Aspects of the Image of God

God wills to have on earth a true reflection of His own character. Specific qualities of God's character appear in us, but we should recognize that the present condition of humankind is not what it was at first. God created Adam good and upright (Genesis 1:31; Ecclesiastes 7:29). But Adam and all his descendants fell into sin. That seriously marred the divine image. Though the divine image has been marred, we continue to reflect, to some extent, the likeness to God. The Bible says little about how glorious was the image of God in Adam before he sinned, but there are clues in Scripture that provide insight regarding the original divine image.

A. Righteousness and Holiness

Having the divine image means Adam was created good and upright. As man came from the hands of God, he was holy and righteous. This truth is implied in Genesis 3, where the Bible tells that Adam fell from a higher moral state to a lower one. At first Adam had a moral likeness to God. "God made man upright, but they have sought out many schemes" (Ecclesiastes 7:29). When Adam sinned, he lost the aspect of the divine image that is holy and righteous. Paul recognized that man's moral likeness to God has been lost, for he said, "Be renewed in the spirit of your mind, and . . . put on the new man which was created according to God, in righteousness and true holiness" (Ephesians 4:23, 24). Sin has adversely affected all of human nature. All the aspects of the image of God in man were weakened, and the entire human personality needs renewal by the

Holy Spirit. Holiness and righteousness, in which the first Adam was created, can only be restored by the second Adam, who is Jesus Christ. The Holy Spirit renews the believer in holiness. Holiness and righteousness from the Holy Spirit, in the Christian, reflect the holiness and righteousness of God in which Adam was created. Moral likeness to God is restored through regeneration and sanctification.

B. Dominion Over Creation Under God

Adam was given dominion over the earth (Genesis 1:27, 28). His authority, for example, was evident in his naming the animals. God shared His sovereignty with him. Of course, Adam's rule was under the rule of God. After proclaiming the greatness of God, the psalmist spoke of man's exalted position under God: "For You [God] have made him [man] a little lower than the angels, and You have crowned him with glory and honor. You have made him to have dominion over the works of Your hands; You have put all things under his feet, all sheep and oxen—even the beasts of the field, the birds of the air, and the fish of the sea that pass through the paths of the seas" (Psalm 8:5-8). Humankind's dominion could not be stated more forcefully. But because of sin, humans have failed to exercise good stewardship over the creation. The Book of Hebrews reminds us that God's intention for us has not been fully realized. After citing Psalm 8:4-6, the writer of Hebrews added, "But now we do not yet see all things put under him [man]" (2:8). Sin has diminished mankind's rule of the creation. As a result, all things are not subject to man. Only through Jesus Christ will the dominion of humankind be restored. While the universal rule of believers is not yet apparent, Christ, who tasted death for everyone, has been enthroned at the right hand of God. His exaltation identified Him as the One "crowned with glory and honor" (2:9).

Therefore He is destined to exercise dominion over the creation. When all things are subjected to Him fully, the redeemed people of God will rule and reign with Him. Then they will reflect the pristine image of God.

C.   The Power to Choose Between Good and Evil

God created Adam as a free, responsible being. Freedom is fundamental to the image of God in which Adam was created. He had the power for moral judgment and choice. He knew right from wrong and could act accordingly. God desired him to obey willingly. Adam was forbidden to eat of "the tree of the knowledge of good and evil" (Genesis 2:17). But because he possessed freedom, he could respond either in obedience or rebellion. He misused his God-given freedom and chose evil rather than good. Through sin he lost his freedom to do only good and became a servant of sin.

Sin has marred the image of God in every person, weakening our power to do good and to avoid evil: "For what I will to do, that I do not practice; but what I hate, that I do" (Romans 7:15). Again we are reminded of the weakness of the human will in these words: "For the flesh lusts against the Spirit, and the Spirit against the flesh; and these are contrary to one another, so that you do not do the things that you wish" (Galatians 5:17). Without God no one has sufficient strength to please Him consistently. Only by the renewing grace of the Holy Spirit, and by walking in the Spirit, is the human will strengthened so that we can exercise our freedom to do good for the glory of God (Romans 8:1-10; Galatians 5:16-18, 25).

D.   Knowledge

A part of God's image in Adam was knowledge. Being in

the likeness of God, he was to walk in knowledge, that is, in the way of truth. God declared His truth to Adam in the Garden of Eden, saying, "Of every tree of the garden you may freely eat; but of the tree of the knowledge of good and evil you shall not eat, for in the day that you eat of it you shall surely die" (Genesis 2:16, 17). These words were the words of God and therefore absolutely true.

If Adam had heeded God's truth, he would have continued to reflect the image in which he was created. But he failed to heed the word of God and to walk in truth. As a consequence, Adam and all his descendants would need to be restored to a state of true knowledge. Such knowledge was an aspect of the image of God before the fall of Adam. Paul reminded the early Christians that they had "put on the new man who is renewed in knowledge according to the image of Him who created him" (Colossians 3:10). For them to have been "renewed in knowledge" meant that they were brought back to a former condition of Adam. By Christ, and only by Him, are we restored to a state of true knowledge. The image of God was marred by sin, but now renewed in Christ we are to walk in truth. That is what Adam did before the Fall. Our renewal in Christ calls us to walk in the full integrity of what God has declared.

E. Immortality

The Bible says that only God has immortality (1 Timothy 6:16). This verse means that God is eternal, has life in Himself, and is the One "who gives life to all things" (v. 13). Human immortality is an endowment derived from God. Had Adam not sinned, doubtlessly he would have gained permanent immortality for soul and body. By creating Adam in His image, God did not intend that Adam should die. He endowed the first man with life. Not only was his soul immortal but also his body, because at first it did not carry the seeds of mortality. Death was threatened as punishment for disobedience (Genesis 2:17). This meant both spiritual and physical death. Death entered the world by the sin of Adam (Romans 5:12; 1 Corinthians 15:21, 22). As a consequence, human life is hemmed in by mortality. But Christ came to experience mortality and embraced death on behalf of us. In so doing, He "abolished death and brought life and immortality to light through the gospel" (2 Timothy 1:10). Through faith in His redemptive work, everlasting life is restored to believers, and eventually our body will be conformed completely to His glorious body (Philippians 3:21).

The Image of God for Those in Christ

The image of God in all of us has been distorted and marred by sin. As sinners, we are in need of spiritual renewal. Through Christ the children of God experience renewal and have solid hope of full and complete transformation into the likeness of God. The basis for such hope is that God sent the God-Man, Jesus Christ, who is the very image of the invisible God (Colossians 1:15; 2 Corinthians 4:4). Scripture assures believers that "as we have borne the image of the man of dust, we shall also bear the image of the heavenly Man" (1 Corinthians 15:49). The image of the man of dust, though distorted by sin, has been borne by every person. Only those in Christ bear the likeness of the heavenly man. Believers' destiny is to share in the likeness and glory of Christ (Romans 8:29; 5:2). When that is finally realized, our body and spirit will be perfectly conformed to the likeness of Christ.

Complete conformity to the likeness of Christ is the goal of salvation. This dynamic process begins at conversion and will be brought to completion at the resurrection of the redeemed. The image of God was bestowed on Adam. But for those in Christ, the renewal of that image is both a present process and a future goal. Through regeneration and sanctification the image of God in the believer is in the process of renewal. The dynamic process of transformation of believers is clearly taught in Scripture: *You have put off the old nature with its deeds and have put on the new nature which is being renewed in knowledge according to the image of its Creator* (Colossians 3:9, 10, author's paraphrase). *We all, with unveiled face, reflecting the glory of the Lord, are being changed into his image from one degree of glory to another* (2 Corinthians 3:18, author's paraphrase). The new life of the believer, given by the Holy Spirit, begins the renewal of the image of God in the believer.

As Pentecostals know well, "Where the Spirit of the Lord is, there is liberty" (2 Corinthians 3:17). This liberty is the freedom to be what God intended us to be. Apart from Christ we are not free but in bondage to selfish desires. But in the freedom of the Spirit there begins a personal transformation into the image of God, the likeness of Christ. Renewal in the likeness of Christ determines the conduct of believers. Therefore Christians are urged to "put on tender mercies, kindness, humbleness of mind, meekness, longsuffering; bearing with one another, and forgiving one another, if anyone has a complaint against another; even as Christ forgave you, so you also must do. But above all these things put on love, which is the bond of perfection" (Colossians 3:12-14). The Spirit's daily renewal of believers is to affect profoundly our relationships with one another. The congregation of believers is to be a fellowship of the Holy Spirit and of love.

The renewal of our mind and will by the Holy Spirit is to continue until our salvation is fully realized (Romans 8:6, 27). At that time our whole self, body and soul, will be conformed to the image of God and Christ. Our bodies of weakness will be transformed into the likeness of Christ's glorified body. It is in the likeness of Christ that we shall finally awake redeemed.

Three Implications of Our Likeness to God

When Adam sinned he rebelled against God and his own true nature. His sin broke fellowship with God and scarred the image of God. So when we examine ourselves, it becomes clear that we are not what God intended us to be. Not only has sin cut us off from God, but it has also distorted our true humanity. Still, the fact that God created humans in His image has important implications.

A. Unique Relationship

In the image of God, we are endowed with the capacity for communion with the Creator that other creatures do not have. To truly live is to live in communion with God. Our attitude toward God determines our relationship with Him. Should our attitude be wrong, then our relationship to Him is wrong. As sinners we stand in a wrong relationship to God; but as people renewed in the image of Christ, we stand in a right relationship with Him. Never did God intend for us to live in isolation. As human beings in the image of God, we are to live in community not only with God but also with one another. We are naturally dependent on one another. We need to give help to others, and we also need their help.

B. Representatives of God

An image can be manufactured to represent a man, animal, or a so-called god. God made us in His image, and thus we are His representatives. And we are to be living reflections of His glory and love. The Most High God is best represented by human beings who are renewed in His image. Rightly, Pentecostals have understood themselves to be representatives of God. Their answer to the question "Who am I?" centers in the scriptural teaching that (1) human beings are made in the image of the Creator and (2) through experienced transformation by the Holy Spirit into the likeness of Christ, they have become a community of the Spirit. Their identity as people of God rests on the biblical doctrine that human beings are created in the image of God, renewed through faith in Christ, and empowered by the Holy Spirit.

C.   Responsibility to God

To be human beings in the image of God makes us responsible to God. As His representatives He requires us to exercise responsible stewardship. That assumes that we have freedom of will and the capacity for moral choice. We are always responsible to God, even though the image in which He made us has been distorted by sin. This truth reminds us that God has something for us to do in the world. He commands us to live a faithful, responsible life in all religious, business, sexual, civic, and social relationships. The image of God in which we were created and which has been renewed in Christ means strength and power to obey and please God, to exercise dominion on the earth under His lordship, to wait on the Lord, to have communion with God and our fellows, to worship Him, and to live and walk in the Spirit. That is the way to live a responsible life and fulfill our humanity in His image.

SELECTED BIBLIOGRAPHY
PART ONE
SCRIPTURES AND REVELATION

Boettner, Loraine. *The Inspiration of the Scriptures*. Grand Rapids: Eerdmans Publishing Co., 1937.

Brown, James D. "The Authority of the Word." *Conference on the Holy Spirit Digest*, Vol. 1. Edited by Gwen Jones. Springfield, Mo.: Gospel Publishing House, 1983.

Bruce, F.F. *Are the New Testament Documents Reliable?* Grand Rapids: Eerdmans, 1954.

Ellis, Earle E. *Paul's Use of the Old Testament*. Grand Rapids: Wm. B. Eerdmans Publishing Co., 1957.

Henry, Carl F.H., ed. *Basic Christian Doctrines*. New York: Holt, Rinehart and Winston, 1962.

Horton, Stanley M. "Why the Bible Is Reliable." *Conference on the Holy Spirit Digest*, Vol. 1. Edited by Gwen Jones. Springfield, Mo.: Gospel Publishing House, 1983.

Lloyd-Jones, D.M. *Authority*. Carlisle, Pa.: Banner of Truth, 1958.

McLean, Mark D. "Toward a Pentecostal Hermeneutic." *Toward a Pentecostal-Charismatic Theology*, 1984 Society for Pentecostal Studies papers.

Menzies, William W. "Biblical Hermeneutics." *Conference on the Holy Spirit Digest*, Vol. 1. Edited by Gwen Jones. Springfield, Mo.: Gospel Publishing House, 1983.

Metzger, Bruce M. *The Canon of the New Testament*. New York:

Oxford University Press, 1987.

Moody, Dale. *The Word of Truth*. Grand Rapids: Wm. B. Eerdmans Publishing Co., 1981.

Moore, Rick D. "A Pentecostal Approach to Scripture." Church of God School of Theology's *Seminary Viewpoint* (November 1987), pp. 4-11.

Moore, Rick D. "Approaching God's Word Biblically: A Pentecostal Perspective." *Old and New Issues in Pentecostalism*, 1989 Society for Pentecostal Studies papers, pp. J1-J5.

Morris, Leon. *I Believe in Revelation*. Grand Rapids: Wm. B. Eerdmans Publishing Co., 1977.

Murray, John. "Systematic Theology." *Westminster Theological Journal*, No. 25 (1963), pp. 133-42.

Niebuhr, Helmut Richard. *The Meaning of Revelation*. New York: The Macmillan Company, 1941.

Patterson, Bob E. "Revelation and the Bible." *Perspectives in Religious Studies* 14, 4 (1987), pp. 19-30.

Stibbs, A.M. *Understanding God's Word*. Wheaton, Ill.: Shaw Publishers, 1976.

Tasker, R.V.G. *Our Lord's Use of the Old Testament*. London: Westminster Chapel, 1953.

Temple, William. *Revelation*. Edited by John Baille and Hugh Martin. New York: Macmillan Company, 1937.

Walvoord, John W., ed. *Inspiration and Interpretation*. Grand Rapids: Wm. B. Eerdmans Publishing Co., 1957.

Wenham, J.W. *Christ and the Bible*. Downers Grove, Ill.: Intervarsity Press, 1972.

Young, Edward J. *The Word Is Truth*. Grand Rapids: Wm. B. Eerdmans Publishing Co., 1957.

SELECTED BIBLIOGRAPHY
PART TWO
DOCTRINE OF GOD

Bloesch, Donald G. *Essentials of Evangelical Theology*, Vol. I: *God, Authority, and Salvation*. San Francisco: Harper and Row Publishers, 1978; pp. 24-50.

Boice, James M. *Our Sovereign God*. Grand Rapids: Baker Book House, 1977.

Brandt, R.L. "The Doctrine of the Trinity." *Conference on the Holy Spirit Digest*, Vol. 1. Edited by Gwen Jones. Springfield, Mo.: Gospel Publishing House, 1983; pp. 82-88.

Brumback, Carl. *God in Three Persons*. Cleveland, Tenn.: Pathway Press, 1959.

Carter, Charles W., ed. *A Contemporary Wesleyan Theology*, Vol. 1. Grand Rapids: Zondervan Publishing House, 1983; pp. 107-236, 375-414.

Clark, Elijah Columbus. *Elohim, or the Manifestation of the Godhead*. Cleveland, Tenn.: Church of God Publishing House, 1920.

Duggan, Michael W. "The Centrality of the Cross for the Baptism in the Spirit." *Toward a Pentecostal-Charismatic Theology*, 1984 Society for Pentecostal Studies papers.

English, E. Schuyler. *Things Surely to Be Believed: A Primer of Bible Doctrine*, Vol. 1. Wheaton, Ill.: Van Kampen Press, 1946; pp. 18-30, 153-177.

Erickson, Millard J. *Christian Theology.* Grand Rapids: Baker Book House, 1985.

Gause, R.H. *The Lukan Transfiguration Account.* Dissertation submitted to Emory University, Atlanta, 1975.

Gordon, A.J. *The Ministry of the Spirit.* Minneapolis, Minn.: Bethany Fellowship, 1964.

Henry, Carl F.H., ed. *Revelation and the Bible.* Grand Rapids: Baker Book House, 1958.

Henry, Carl F.H. *God, Revelation and Authority,* Vols. V & VI; *God Who Stands and Stays,* Parts I & II. Waco, Texas: Word Books Publisher, 1983.

McClung, Floyd Jr. *The Father Heart of God.* Eugene, Ore.: Harvest House Publishers, 1971.

Menzies, William W. "The Holy Spirit in Christian Theology." *Perspectives on Evangelical Theology.* Edited by Kenneth S. Kantzer and Stanley N. Gundry. Grand Rapids: Baker Book House, 1979.

Pearlman, Myer. *Knowing the Doctrines of the Bible.* Springfield, Mo.: Gospel Publishing House, 1937; pp. 33-80, 90-137.

Pink, Arthur W. *The Attributes of God.* Grand Rapids: Baker Book House, 1975.

Reeves, Kenneth V. *The Godhead.* Granite City, Ill.: K.V. Reeves, 1984.

Spittler, Russel P. *God the Father.* Springfield, Mo.: Gospel Publishing House, 1976.

Storms, C. Samuel. *The Grandeur of God: A Theological and Devotional Study of the Divine Attributes.* Grand Rapids: Baker Book House, 1984.

Synan, J.A. *The Trinity, or the Tri-Personal Being of God.* Franklin Springs, Ga.: Advocate Press, 1980.

Torrey, R.A. *The Person and Work of the Holy Spirit.* Grand Rapids: Zondervan, 1910.

Tozer, A.W. *The Knowledge of the Holy.* Lincoln, Neb.: Back to the Bible Broadcast, 1961.

Wiley, H. Orton. *Christian Theology,* Vol. 2. Kansas City, Mo.: Hill Press, 1966; pp. 7-52.

Williams, J. Rodman. *Renewal Theology: God, the World, and Redemption.* Grand Rapids: Zondervan, 1988; pp. 29-116, 197-220.

Williams, J. Rodman. "A Pentecostal Theology." *The Distinctiveness of Pentecostal-Charismatic Theology,* 1985 Society for Pentecostal Studies papers.

Wright, J. Stafford. *Understanding Bible Teaching: God's Character.* Grand Rapids: Eerdmans, 1972.

SELECTED BIBLIOGRAPHY
PART THREE
DOCTRINE OF CREATION

Ackerman, Paul D. *It's a Young World After All: Exciting Evidences for Recent Creation.* Grand Rapids: Baker Book House, 1986.

Anderson, Susan. *Creation in Eschatological Tension: A Premise of Pauline Theodicy,* 1979.

Bonhoeffer, Dietrich. *Creation and Fall: A Theological Interpretation of Genesis 1-3.* Translated by John C. Fletcher. New York: Macmillan, 1959.

Flamming, Peter James. *God and Creation.* Nashville: Broadman Press, 1985.

Florovsky, Georges. *Creation and Redemption.* Belmont, Mass.: Nordland Publishing Co., 1976.

Gibbs, John G. *Creation and Redemption: A Study in Pauline Theology.* Leiden, Netherlands: Brill, 1971.

Gish, Duane T. *Evolution: The Fossils Say No!* San Diego: Creation-Life Publishers, 1978.

Houston, J.M. *I Believe in the Creator.* Grand Rapids: Eerdmans, 1980.

Moltmann, Jurgen. *God in Creation: A New Theology of Creation and the Spirit of God: The Gifford Lectures, 1984-1985.* San Francisco: Harper and Row, 1985.

Morris, Henry M., and Duane T. Gish, editors. *The Battle for Creation: Acts/Facts/Impacts*, Vol. 2. San Diego: Creation-Life Publishers, 1976.

Morris, Henry M. *The Scientific Case for Creation*. San Diego: Creation-Life Publishers, 1977.

Newell, Philip Rutherford. *Light out of Darkness: The Six Days of Creation and the Problem of Evolution*. Chicago: Moody Press, n.d.

Newman, Robert Chapman. *Genesis One & the Origin of the Earth*. Downers Grove, Ill.: Intervarsity Press, 1977.

Rehwinkel, Alfred Martin. *The Wonders of Creation: an Exploration of the Origin and Splendors of the Universe*. Minneapolis: Bethany Fellowship, 1974.

Van Till, Howard J., et. al. *Portraits of Creation: Biblical and Scientific Perspectives on the World's Formation*. Grand Rapids: Wm. B. Eerdmans Publishing Co., 1990.

Walker, Paul L. *Understanding the Bible and Science*. Cleveland, Tenn.: Pathway Press, 1976.

Young, Norman James. *Creator, Creation, and Faith*. Philadelphia: Westminster Press, 1976.

SELECTED BIBLIOGRAPHY
PART FOUR
DOCTRINE OF MAN

Babbage, Stuart Barton. *Man in Nature and in Grace.* Grand Rapids: Eerdmans, 1957.

Brunner, Emil. *Man in Revolt: A Christian Anthropology.* Translated by Olive Wyon. Philadelphia: Westminster Press, 1947.

Burns, J. Patout. *Theological Anthropology.* Philadelphia: Fortress Press, 1981.

Custance, Arthur C. *Genesis and Early Man.* Grand Rapids: Zondervan Publishing House, 1975.

Custance, Arthur C. *Man in Adam and in Christ.* Grand Rapids; Zondervan Publishing House, 1979.

Gundry, Robert Horton. *Soma in Biblical Theology: With Emphasis on Pauline Anthropology.* Cambridge: Cambridge University Press, 1976.

Harris, R. Laird. *Man—God's Eternal Creation: Old Testament Teaching on Man and His Culture.* Chicago: Moody Press, 1971.

Inch, Morris A. *Psychology in the Psalms: A Portrait of Man in God's World.* Waco, Texas: Word Books, 1969.

Machen, J. Gresham. *The Christian View of Man.* Grand Rapids: Wm. B. Eerdmans, 1947.

Macquarrie, John. *In Search of Humanity: A Theological and Philosophical Approach.* New York: Crossroad, 1983.

Pitman, Michael. *Adam and Evolution: A Scientific Critique of Neo-Darwinism*. Grand Rapids: Baker Book House, 1987.

Robinson, H. Wheeler. *The Christian Doctrine of Man*. Third edition. Edinburgh: T. & T. Clark, 1926.

Sauer, Erich. *The King of the Earth: The Nobility of Man According to the Bible and Science*. Grand Rapids: Eerdmans, 1962.

Shedd, Russell Philip. *Man in Community: A Study of St. Paul's Application of Old Testament and Early Jewish Conceptions of Human Solidarity*. Grand Rapids: Eerdmans, 1964.

Stedman, Ray C. *Understanding Man*. Waco, Texas: Word Books, 1975.

White, William Luther. *The Image of Man in C.S. Lewis*. Nashville: Abingdon Press, 1969.

Wood, Arthur Skevington. *The Nature of Man*. Grand Rapids: Wm. B. Eerdmans, 1978.

Notes

Notes

Notes

Notes

Notes

Notes

Notes

Notes

Notes

Notes

Notes

Notes

Notes

Notes

Notes

Notes

Notes

Notes

Notes

Notes

Notes

Notes

Notes

Notes

Notes

Notes

Notes

Notes

Notes

Notes

Notes

Notes

Notes

Notes

Notes

Notes

Notes

Notes

Notes

Notes

Notes

Notes

Notes

Notes

Notes

Notes